This is a book for our time; written with conscientious compassion and Feminine wisdom—a thinking woman's call to awaken a shared consciousness that is our power. Kayta, like Adrienne Rich, understands that compassion is not passive; that compassion should ignite passion for change and for truth.

Colleen O'Connell, Chief Administrative Officer, Won Institute of Graduate Studies

When Kathleen sent me this book, I expected to simply browse the content and share my opinion. Boy was I surprised when I read the first few chapters and couldn't wait to read the rest of the book, every page of it. Filled with compelling and important information that we all need to read, digest, understand, learn from. And live with!

Please read this book, it will help you awaken to a new way of looking at the truth of our lives.

Dr. Dan Gottlieb, Psychologist and Host of Voices in the Family

Dr. Gajdos ... with an informed, passionate, and incisive voice articulates the outrages against the feminine principle which have governed the Western world for so many centuries. The reader might be made uncomfortable by her critique, even defensive, but try to refute her, and then one finds her "quiet wisdom" accurate, prophetic, and embracing the only path for healing our broken world, our sundered psyches.

Dr. James Hollis, J̣ .... *such books as* What Matters Mo .... Life

Kayta has given us a touching but hard-hitting look at what it is like to be a woman in a society of domination. We come to see, in poignant and well-documented ways, just how slow we and our leaders have been to institute equality for the sexes. This book can launch us on a journey: We can recognize the wounds we have so often overlooked and then commit ourselves to acknowledge, undo, and heal them.
David Richo, Ph.D., Author of How to be an Adult in Love *(Shambhala, 2014)*

Awakening ourselves to the wounded feminine, through Dr. Gajdos' thought-provoking writing, is an important step towards making the church whole.
Joan Wylie, Deacon, Episcopal Diocese of Pennsylvania

In these loud times it's good to hear the quiet voice of Kayta Gajdos calling our attention to the wounded feminine. Against a backdrop of contemporary issues, this insightful and experienced Jungian informed psychologist confronts the perennial enigma of the balance of masculine and feminine energies, to arrive at what she terms "a heartful mind." She is indeed a woman of heart who needs to be heard!
Patty de Llosa, Author of Taming Your Inner Tyrant

Written eloquently in a perceptive woman's clear and conscious voice, *Quiet Wisdom in Loud Times* raises our awareness to the grave danger we face as a species if we fail to reinstate the feminine in her rightful place, not only in our minds, but more importantly in our hearts. ... Kayta Curzie

Gajdos presents a compelling picture of how we devalue the feminine in our society and how we, both men and women, can rectify this through the thoughtful application of spiritual principles in our lives.

Russill Paul, Author of The Yoga of Sound: Tapping the Hidden Power of Music and Chant

... Dr. Gajdos' message comes, at a time when our world, politically, religiously and relationally is so divided. Yet, over that destructive din, she explores the quiet rumblings of compassion and creativity that are emerging. [...] She writes meaningfully from the personal to the global and our need to embrace a compassionate, constructive path that will unify us.

Marie Hulse Cowan, LMFT, Marriage and Family Therapist

[Dr. Kayta Curzie Gajdos' *Quiet Wisdom in Loud Times*] is like a drink of fresh, cool water on a hot day. Her book brings so much heartfelt wisdom into life's noise and shrillness. Dr. Gajdos has sought, successfully, to help bring peace to all of us, male and female, but particularly to the women who often bear the responsibility of managing humankind's countless villages. As a long-time peace activist and professional peace-maker, Dr. Gajdos has brought together her many and varied experiences, broad knowledge, and memorable observations into a book that can help all of us find our own inner peace, as well as strive for peace among nations.

Karen Porter, Director, The Chester County Peace Movement

Dr. Kayta Gajdos [...] enables the reader to understand how the feminine archetype has been "wounded" and how we—men, women, and our planet itself—will benefit from a re-balancing of these two principles. Dr. Gajdos has issued a clarion call to awaken and to take action, for if we are to survive, our inter-connectedness and compassion must be honored and restored.

George Leute, Psychologist and Dream Worker

... a great ride through some pretty complex territory...

JanStephen Cavanaugh, Ph.D., President, Global Human Development, Inc.

QUIET WISDOM IN LOUD TIMES

QUIET WISDOM IN LOUD TIMES

THE RISE OF THE WOUNDED FEMININE

KAYTA CURZIE GAJDOS, PH.D.

BRANDYWINE CREEK PRESS

CHADDS FORD, PENNSYLVANIA

First Printing, 2014

ISBN-13: 978-0-9915566-0-1
ISBN-10: 0-9915566-0-7
E-Book ISBN-13: 978-0-9915566-1-8
E-Book ISBN-10: 0-9915566-1-5
Library of Congress Control Number: 2014904777

BRANDYWINE
CREEK PRESS

Chadds Ford, Pennsylvania
United States of America

Cover Photo: Hawai`i Volcanoes National Park, 2010. Photo by the author.

CONTENTS

FOREWORD

In this age of seemingly endless uncontrollable violence there is a desperate need for change, for a balancing force, for a return to sanity.

Dr. Gajdos points out in powerful memorable words and images that the world is out of balance. She is optimistic that there is a force in the world today that will restore balance that is desperately needed. The force she writes about is the rise of the wounded feminine.

Every night on TV and in our movies we see countless acts of cruelty, torture and murder. They fascinate us. We see the "heroes" of these works as men (usually) to be admired and emulated for their power. But in another sense what are we presenting to the world and to our children. Do they only resonate and emulate that good will triumph over evil? Do they not also admire and emulate the power and the violence and the invincibility of these murdering heroes?

Seen in this light our movie and television industries are pumping poison into the minds of our children – and people and children all over the world. Is it any surprise then to read every other week of another shooting in a school, another rampage in a mall, another group of children murdered by a disturbed violent man with an assault weapon and hundreds of rounds of ammunition?

One of the images that Dr. Gajdos recalls for us is of Lisbeth Salander of the Girl with the Dragon Tattoo. The image presented on the screen is of Lisbeth, after her father and brother have beaten and buried her in the backyard. Out of the dirt that was thrown on her grave, we see her hand slowly emerge and reach upward to the sky. This is the rise of the wounded feminine. This is what the world needs.

As a society we have elevated the masculine traits and denigrated the feminine traits. We must restore the feminine qualities.

In this beautifully written book Dr. Gajdos gives us many instances of the masculine domination and where that has taken us and where it will lead us in the future. She also gives us examples of women and men in whom the feminine qualities and traits exist. She tells us of their accomplishments and their goals and explains very clearly why they are a force for good in the world

Her analysis of Stieg Larsson's trilogy, based on a Jungian perspective, is a brilliant example of her overall thesis.

She also explores the meaning of many current events:

The rise of Hillary Clinton, Meg Whitman, Judge Ruth Bader Ginsburg; The TV series The Good Wife and The Newsroom; The movies The Hunger Games; The Help, The Color Purple and The Whale Rider; The buying of America by the Koch brothers and others; The Catholic Church today; the turmoil in the Israeli-Palestinian Conflict; our

Supreme Court and many other organizations and aspects of everyone's life.

The world has committed violence against women. We celebrate and reward the masculine and we denigrate and repress the feminine. We are the worse for it. Suggestions for the control of violence more often than not are based on further male domination: "Arm the teachers." "More police", "Metal detectors everywhere". "Give the peaceful people more powerful weapons to counterattack the attackers". "Meet force with more force." A Texas politician actually suggested that if everyone in the theater, where the Batman movie played, had been "packing heat" the killer would have been shot before he killed so many people. Really? And what about the bullets flying around the theater – hundreds and hundreds of bullets fired wildly by panicked frightened people? How many in that theater would have been shot by all of those who were "packing' heat"?

Where will this take us?

Gandhi asked, "Where does 'an eye for an eye' lead us? It leads us to a world in which everyone is blind."

Are we already blind?

This is an important book that should be read far and wide. It is a call for sanity in a world gone mad with the thirst for power, money, revenge, violence and murder. We are poisoning our children, poisoning our rivers, poisoning our sky and poisoning the Earth.

Dr. Gajdos's book is a call to arms. Her message is, *We must lay down our arms, our assault weapons, our rifles our handguns and we must reach out our arms...to embrace each other.*

We live in a world in which the masculine is dominant and the feminine is repressed. Our world is out of balance. To survive we must change.

Barry M. Panter, M.D., Ph.D.
Founder and Co-Director,
The American Institute of Medical Education
The Creativity and Madness Conferences
Diplomate,
The American Board of Psychiatry and Neurology
Author,
33 Poems for Mary Lou

COMMENTARY

Quiet Wisdom in Loud Times: The Rise of the Wounded Feminine can be thought of as a must read for anyone interested in the feminist movement and how much wonderful good has been brought to humanity to date by feminism, and leads the reader into thinking about "what's next".

To all male readers, you will hear her saying it's not ALL your fault, we all are "like a school of fish in the waters" and that "Patriarchal power is in the air we breathe ..." Her message: We are in this mess together, and only together will we get out of it.

From the perspective of human development with the focus on positive human potential what she is proposing is exactly "right on" in terms of what needs to happen for humanity to rise to an integrated and fully equated sex and gender level of psychic functioning. She most of all reminds us that we live in critical times and that what we are doing now will greatly impact our great, great grandchildren. We can see through her eyes how this imbalance at this time in human history is leading us to the age of catastrophe. It is a truism of human development that any system that gets "way out of balance with systems of feedback behind the curve" will self-destruct.

From the view of this man, her call to give life to the wounded feminine rising that I might heal, gave me a pause to reflect on how and what I need to do in support of the wounded masculine rising in me. What world might come about when women are in animus balance and men in anima balance? I suggest that will be Patriarchy Transformed and with that the Age of Peace can be upon us.

Her message, "Wake Up".

JanStephen Cavanaugh, Ph.D.
President,
Global Human Development, Inc.

DEDICATION

When late afternoon light lit upon a piece of crystal in my office window, I mused, "I should write my mother's memoirs." Later I expanded the thought of her memoirs and started writing and presenting, *Quiet Wisdom in Loud Times: Women of Heart Who Need to Heard.* Well, this book is neither my mother's memoirs nor is it solely about women of heart. It is about healing the woundedness of the feminine principle which is buried in us all. It is well nigh time for her resurrection.

Nevertheless, I would like to dedicate this book to my mother (while, at the same time, not forgetting my grandmothers before her, and my children who are heirs of her heart and soul—quintessential grandmother that she was.)

Now that I have some distance on the family of origin dynamics, and my mother and her sisters have all died, I am beginning to view her story—"herstory"—as one more saga of women having to defer to a patriarchal culture. She quit high school in order to work so her brothers could continue their education. Stymied by the patriarchal system, she nevertheless accepted its norms, deferring to the men in her midst, doting on my older brother (big brother disagrees), seeking affirmation from her highly successful younger brother (she never got it). Even though my father, for a 1950's husband was pretty mild as patriarchs go, he still controlled her life. She seemed in the dark as to their financial problems and didn't learn to drive a car until she was in her late forties (and she never did get to learn to ride a bicycle!).

I think of Maxine Hong Kingston's book, *Woman Warrior*, as converging with my mother's story. King notes, in her memoir, an aunt who was excised from her family in China after she suicided. My mother also had a sister pushed off the family tree, perhaps for similar reasons. The ghosts in both cases remain. Might this book honor these shadows as well? The forgotten and dismissed wounded feminine!

Of course, it is not women and girls alone who are dismissed and denigrated by the lack of feminine principle. When a boy is raped by teammates and a community coalesces to support the perpetrators (who also need help!) with the refrain, "boys will be boys," we see violence institutionalized and condoned once again—a burial of the feminine principle.

So it is that our society still must evolve in order not to devolve. We cannot point a finger at other cultures when we sometimes do so poorly in our own.

There is hope if we honor the feminine principle of relationship and connection in us all. So it is that I look forward to the <u>day</u> when a feminine principled woman is in the White House as a matter of course, not considered a crisis, and I look forward to the <u>night</u> when women can freely walk alone and unafraid.

WHY THIS BOOK NOW?

The loss of feminine qualities and energy is an urgent psychological issue in modern society. It is a painful concern in the emotional lives of both men and women. (Johnson, Femininity Lost and Regained, p 1.)

When I began writing, 2010 was dubbed the year of the conservative woman by several news organizations. California Republicans nominated Meg Whitman and Carly Fiorina, Connecticut conservatives nominated Linda McMahon for Senate, and Delaware nominated Christine O'Donnell. Later, Nikki Haley was elected the GOP governor of South Carolina. In a Los Angeles Times article entitled, "2010: The Year of the Conservative Woman?" Doyle McManus noted, "newly chosen female nominees show that the GOP primary voters, a deeply conservative bunch, don't appear to have a problem with strong women in public life anymore."

(June 10, 2010) In other words, Republicans appeared to accept that a woman's place was not only in the home but also in the House (or Senate).

Writing this book in the midst of sea changes one minute and the rolling back of the tide in the next has been a dizzying experience for which Dramamine is no antidote. Because, as much as 2010 seemed to be a victory of the daughters of the patriarchy, 2012's rallying cry became, "Stop the Republican war on women!"

Suddenly, women's reproductive rights, not to mention childcare and equal pay, became the boiling cauldrons on the front burners. When President Obama's health care bill was to be enacted, and would include contraception coverage even in religiously affiliated hospitals, the lines were drawn. Those I term the conservative patriarchs, were camped against the health care bill in general, and the contraception package in particular. On the other side, women and feminine principled men, spoke out in favor of the health care bill as well as the contraception prescription benefits. Meanwhile, Representative Todd Akin will forever be known for his comments about how, in "legitimate" rape, a woman's body defends against getting pregnant. Another of his conservative cohorts, Richard Mourdock, later expounded that, if there is a pregnancy as the result of rape, it is an act of God. So the issue of abortion in harsh economic times became even more focal in politics—if that is possible!

Well, these comments backfired—many women were activated to vote both for the liberal women running for office as well as for the re-election of President Obama. And so it is that Clair McCaskill defeated Todd Akin in Missouri's US Senate race.

Nevertheless, the saga continues and the sea change is not set.

WHY THIS TOPIC— QUIET WISDOM IN LOUD TIMES: THE RISE OF THE WOUNDED FEMININE

For several years now, I have been processing in my head, and meandering on paper, with the phrases, quiet wisdom in loud times: women of heart who need to be heard, the rise of the wounded feminine.

In the midst of my preoccupation with writing a book about "quiet wisdom in loud times: women of heart who need to be heard," I go to the movies. Not in chronological order, but indeed synchronistically, I see "The Girl Who Played with Fire," the Swedish screen adaptation of Stieg Larsson's second book of his trilogy about Lisbeth Salander.

Not a crime fiction fan, I am nevertheless gripped by this heroine. In the finale of the film, I witness her father shoot her, and her half-brother bury her. Then at dawn, her hand rises from the grave. I am stunned: here it is, the rise of the wounded feminine despite patriarchy's destructive violence. This event was larger than Lisbeth.

I considered her attempted murder by a brutal father, and her resurrection despite it, to be the resounding metaphor of our times: we are in a global crisis of an old order of the patriarchy that wants to maintain the status quo of wealth and power. Yet the feminine principle so wounded by the violence against it continues to rise up.

By the wounded feminine principle, I refer to both men and women.

Women have come a long way since the 1960's, but that really isn't the whole story. In fact, the story is not even about women only. It is about men also. It is about something, in fact, beyond both men and women and that is the rise of the wounded feminine soul energy that needs to be part and parcel of all of us. Why now? I think we are at a very important time, where there are huge psychic upheavals happening.

Right now life is still in patriarchal dominator mode. But this is NOT about gender. Women can be daughters of a rigid patriarchal structure as much as men can be its sons. Likewise, men, as well as women, can carry the collaborative, partnership model that attends to the feminine, relational aspects of life.

Every day, I study the news with the perspective of where is the wounded feminine rising, where are the women (and men) of heart? Or, where is it not! When the Supreme Court recently ruled in favor of Walmart over women who claimed discrimination, I thought, "another victory for the patriarchy." I thought that also when I heard the Supreme Court also ruled against the environmental concerns of cities.

These rulings are patriarchal and not integrated with the feminine principle perspective because they are about domination and control rather than concern for the inter-relat-edness and connection of the world.

When the feminine principle is dismissed, the result is rape and violence.

Look what the patriarchy has accomplished not heeding the feminine principle.

For one, pervasive and prolonged sexual abuse crimes within the Catholic Church. The hierarchy exacerbated the tragedy, first by inexcusable denial of it, and then, further, by one cover up after another. Not that the Catholic Church is alone in its actions or lack thereof. Penn State has its own sexual abuse crimes. Again, an old boy network minimized the allegations. The bottom line appeared to be about saving football, saving face, and keeping the money flowing. Concern for the hurt children was hardly a priority. Now, most recently (as of this writing), the Boy Scouts admit to sexual abuse cover ups as well.

But the patriarchy doesn't stop at rape and violence against the powerless—whether they be adults or children. There is also a rape of the earth. Ironically, we refer to our planet as Mother Earth. We rely on her: we need nature to nurture us. However, we patriarchs pillage her as though she were one big village to vanquish and we were the invading victors. Mother Earth is not so powerless, however; and there will be payback for our plunder. We cannot continue to ignore the FACT of climate change with impunity. We cannot, in our myopic vision, deplete natural resources forever. We cannot live without clean water and clean air.

MONTEREY MEANDERINGS

On June 22, 2010, while visiting my son in California, I journaled the following:

I wake up to election news on NPR—the same NPR that awakens me at home, three thousand miles from this Pacific coastal place. They are talking about Haley's election, the Republican woman in the South who has converted from the Sikh religion to Christianity. She proclaims Christ and disavows any talk of her affairs. Her affairs are her affairs—no business of mine. Her conservative politics however are a worry. Again, we have a woman coming to power who I fear will be giving women of compassion a bad name. Now the patriarchy has mesmerized women to do its last gasp bidding. These women don't see how they are betraying the lineage of women who cry for their grandmother's pain, who cry from the Mother Earth we rape. In this, they suffer their own Stockholm syndrome. Indeed, in 2012, Governor Haley cut back funding for rape crisis centers and domestic violence in South Carolina. At the same time, she promoted off shore oil drilling.

The next bit of news on NPR was about the indigenous people of the Amazon who were becoming ill from the oil drilling and the oil spills in their jungle. We humans have done it again. Striking it rich, slowly exterminating the Earth's natives. We all go watch Avatar, rooting for the indigenous of Pandora and then we leave the fantasy realm and make a factory of the Universe.

So lead and cadmium are found in the land and water of the jungle, byproducts of the numerous oil spills in Peru. The indigenous have no say; the Peruvian government gives the green light to the multinational corporations to go pillage the village; the mass weapons of destruction here are dozers and oil rigs. (It is as though

I am spitting into the wind, so much brute, patriarchal power, so much is already polluted that sometimes it seems as though Goliath is winning.) Slowly the people will get sick and die off. Such a subtle death that can be blamed on nutrition and primitive ways—never mind that these folks managed to procreate healthily for thousands of years until now. Pollution and contamination from this oil become the new smallpox. The effect is the same. Eradication of a nation of people. Quiet genocide. The story is told only to be forgotten moments later.

We have creationists believing that dinosaurs walked around the earth just six thousand years ago with us little people. We have corporationists capitalizing on the fossilized remains of cycads and Tyrannosaurus Rex. (Those old enough will remember the Sinclair gas station signs with the dinosaur logo.)

Ah, yes, oil is "natural"—all coming from old earth, except Earth is getting fed up with our plunder. The sacred feminine needs to be respected, heeded. I want to shout to the world boldly, "STOP! NO! You're going the wrong way!" It is one thing to continue to reinvent the wheel. It is far worse to continually fall asleep at the wheel. Wake up world and stop making the same patriarchal mistakes over and over.

Not only is the common good of other peoples not considered when we disregard the feminine principle, we also forget ourselves. The humanitarian notion of the common good relies on a recognition of collaboration, care, and inter-connectedness. That is, an honoring of the feminine principle. Living the lopsided patriarchal view, we are in "macho mania."

We are in an abusive relationship with ourselves. Our feminine principle is getting knocked about by the very abusive patri-

arch that we are married to—come hell or high water (all too literally, given many floods). The greedy patriarch pummels us with tax cuts for the rich and cuts in funding for the rest, especially the poor. Some of us, feeling low self-worth and deserving of violence, keep coming back for more. We vote the abusers back in power. The macho mighty patriarch convinces us that he knows best, that he knows what is good for us. We need to be kept in line, after all. We go to bed with him—sometimes by force—but then there are the kids we have together. Some of the kids buy big Daddy's lies: they want to align with his powerful arm and begin to believe the stories that their feminine principle—mother is a witless wimp wielding no authority. This must change.

If we think we've already changed: the problem of the denigration of women and the wounding of the feminine principle is over there—more fundamentalists in the Middle East or Africa, say—and not here, think again.

SHUTTING WOMEN UP

To bring home to you that our collective unconscious has some serious work to do to become more of a compassionate conscience, allow me to tell you a story that happened recently across the street from my home. Every year my town of Chadds Ford has a community fair to commemorate the Battle of the Brandywine which occurred on September 11, 1777.

However, in 2010, something occurred that I found not only perplexing, but downright disturbing. A volunteer male re-enactor appeared dressed as a woman being punished for "gossip." He, as a colonial woman, wore a metal head covering that disabled speech. Called a brank, or "gossip's bridle," it is described as a "shocking instrument, a sort of iron cage, ... great weight ... with a spiked tongue of iron ... if the offender spoke, she was cruelly hurt."

A man dressed as a woman in colonial garb being punished for being a "gossip". *Photo taken by the author.*

Mind you, this punishment was meant for women who "scolded" or "gossiped"—that is, spoke out in any way in a society in which they had no say. Historians remind us that colonial women had no legal rights as individuals. Judge and jury were all men. What may be one man's being scolded, may be a woman's speaking her truth.

Would that I could now say that the re-enactment of the so-called town gossip stood to remind us of how far we have come from such degrading, humiliating, and cruel treatment of another human being. Unfortunately, the re-enactor's silent stance appears to have become a symbol for some men to long for the "good old days." I was appalled to overhear (ooh, am I gossiping?) one man (who looked, for all intents and purposes, like a regular family man) wax on with some men behind a food counter, "Hey, did you see the guy dressed as a woman gossip?" His words were something to the effect of that's appropriate punishment for a woman.

The group didn't disagree. I later asked one of the men who had taken part in the conversation, "What was that woman gossip stuff all about?" His response was, "Well, it doesn't hurt anybody"—implying that shame and humiliation is a fair and just punishment. His parting comment to me was, "Just don't gossip." (Hmm...)

Later I noticed the "gossip" was in the vicinity again standing silently under a tree. As I was asking the re-enactor if I could take a photo (he nodded assent, not being able to speak), another man walked by, commenting and laughing at how funny the gossip was. Another "Great way to shut a woman up," so to "speak!"

What is so horrifying to me is some men's response to the "village gossip."

Perhaps, these same men watching another man be pilloried or flogged would think that humorous as well as well-deserved. That too would indicate a lack of the feminine principle of compassion. I don't know if this recent experience has more to do with men denigrating women or with the fact that we are all far more primal and less civilized than we'd like to believe. We pride ourselves on liberty and justice for ALL, yet we continue to believe that shame and humiliation and cruel punishment of other human beings will "learn'em."

So the patriarchy is still alive, if (one would hope) not well (Richo, *Mary Within*, p. 41):

> *The dominator [patriarchy] model in relating to women leads to and is based on misogyny. In our society there is a philosophical reverence toward motherhood but often a hatred of actual women. There are people who love the Madonna but are not kind to the women in their lives. It is up to each of us to examine our conscience and confront these contradictions. They usually have roots in our original relationship to our own mothers and require therapy to resolve.*

The Globalization of Abuse

Nicholas Kristof and Sheryl WuDunn, in their book, *Half the Sky: Turning Oppression into Opportunity for Women Worldwide,* talk about female genital cutting. Marti Moss-Coane on Radio Times (February 9, 2011) interviewed the makers of the documentary Mrs. Goundo's Daughter, Barbara Attie and Janet Goldwater, about genital cutting. Apparently this was done to women in Europe in earlier centuries – as recently as the 1860's. It appears to have been practiced for thousands of years – Egyptian mummies have been found with indication of having undergone such clitoral (and other vaginal) mutilation. Another form of control over a woman's sexuality done to insure that she shall not be promiscuous and shall not have pleasure.

Seen as a cultural norm, women accept that the "procedure" must be done to their daughters and granddaughters as well.

While we find these stories appalling, we forget our own Botox Barbie Doll syndrome and the blood on the bulimic ballerina's toes. The women who die from silicone injections to "enhance" their buttocks, the breast implants. These are done because of some societal cultural "norm"or "abnorm" as the case may be. Women and the feminine principle have been either objectified, or denigrated, or dismissed for years. The story continues. But maybe, just maybe, the wounded feminine is rising. That men are becoming empowered not by machismo but by their openness and kindness and receptivity. That women are becoming empowered thrusting forth into the world speaking their truth to patriarchal power.

CHANGE AND CHANGE BACK!

A friend of my daughter, a young woman who works at the state department, questions at dinner why there is such a rise of fundamentalism and a push toward ultra-conservatism. (She remarks, "Why is it that the extreme right wing seems to be on the upswing globally?")

I would say that the backward movement she perceives in the world (and she has traveled much) is the change back response of a global system resisting an evolutionary momentum forward. I have, on the micro level, seen how families call for "change back" whenever an individual in that system moves into a more conscious and aware place. No longer unconscious and drinking the family Kool-Aid that denies the elephant in the living room, the truth teller is anathema to the closed and constricted system that is that particular family's story.

One of my first family cases was where the father had faced his alcoholism and stopped his drinking. His family would have to communicate with him in a new and conscious way, given that he was no longer quietly soused. Quite frankly, they stated their wish that he would change back and drink again.

Being more conscious and engaged may sometimes be "more work" than keeping the status quo. So be it. Resistance and the cry for change back is a great sign that we're going in the right direction. The cry is not a warning about going down a one-way street in the wrong direction; the cry is for keeping the status quo stuck in mud.

So on the one hand, we see how much cry for systemic change back there is. Nostalgia for the good old days. For whom? While fundamentalism and conservatism drives us collectively deeper into the muddy ditch, there is also a push for a larger consciousness. There are women—and men—all over the globe who alert us to change, and who are honoring the feminine principle. We cannot go back, the truth is out, and denial and all the loud shouts for change back can't turn developing consciousness of the rise of the feminine principle, wounded though it has been.

However, we need to begin to see how it is not about

women versus men anymore. Actually it never was. The master is slave to his slavery, and the greedy choke on their gold. How can one half of humanity be out of balance without the other half being off kilter as well. Remember being on a teeter-totter or seesaw? If the weight is not balanced on the two sides, it is hard to go anywhere. And if there is not cooperation by both sides, there is no joy of movement.

Men and women are neither from Mars nor Venus but are from this one Earth. What nonsense gets pandered to prolong the patriarchy's passing. It needs to die for new life to emerge: the arising feminine principle has been wounded for thousands of years. This is about balance and integration, not hostile takeover.

The women's movement brought into focus how unbalanced we have been—and still are—regarding the welfare of women. Feminists, both men and women, also see that all humanity must be treated with fairness, justice, and mercy. And so the corollary to feminism is indeed multiculturalism and diversity.

Terrorist and white supremacist Anders Breivik, in his manifesto, railed against the feminists because of this: he understood how important the feminist movement and I dare say the feminine principle, was and is to inclusiveness and acceptance of the so-called other. Unfortunately, rather than seeing this as a transformational movement to change the course of history, Breivik and other patriarchs of his ilk fear that this change will portend the downfall of their reign—sometimes of terror.

In August, 2011, I wrote the following in my *Mind Matters* Column (ChaddsFordLive.com):

As I was driving last week, I caught the news on the radio that there had been a bombing in Oslo, Norway of a government building ... next, the reporter presumes, with no evidence, that the perpetrator of this crime must indeed be a Muslim jihadist-terrorist. I immediately, as I am wont to do, yelled back at my dashboard, "No! This sounds like a white, right-wing extremist to me." This same man, Anders Behring Breivik, soon after the explosion, massacred children and families at a summer camp.

Once the murderer was identified, no one called him a terrorist, but a lone madman. He may have acted alone, but his profoundly disturbed thinking arises from a milieu of fear and hatred that spews forth from many a media personality as well as from a certain "genre" (that nomenclature is undeserved) of writers—some of whom even purport to be Christian.

Note that Breivik castigated women: in his 1500-page manifesto, he decried the feminist movement for leading us into the multiculturalism that would be the downfall of the white male. Fortunately, not every man (white, or otherwise) who longs for the continuance of the patriarchy's stronghold is prone to violence.

However, when we wish to keep others down or persist in thinking that any "race" (a bogus genetic issue anyway: there is more genetic difference within a given "race" that there is between "races") is better than any other, or that men are of a superior gender, we <u>do engender</u> violence.

My Personal Experience of the Wounded Feminine

Later, in August, 2011, there was an earthquake that shook

practically the entire eastern seaboard of the United States. That evening, my husband, becoming more and more a man who embodies the feminine principle, his anima, with ease, turned on an HBO special about Gloria Steinem. She, along with other women of the 1960's and 1970's, shook the world as well. Then, the hue and cry was to awaken consciousness to the fact that women were treated as second-class. In the earlier part of the century women had fought hard for the right to vote, but that was hardly the end to it. Women were still in the 1970's thwarted in their own lives. A bachelor's degree was more a wife decree, a means for those luck enough, to become a Mrs. Ornament for one of the many "Madmen" (alas, the TV program I cannot bear to watch because of its accurate portrayal of those times).

My own history gives testimony to the times. While I was admitted to the only all women's medical school in the U.S. in 1967 (Woman's Medical College in Philadelphia), all the other medical schools accepted only one to three (if at all) women to their one hundred men. In 1972, I was told flat out that my earning capacity did not count a whit for procuring a mortgage. Quite bluntly, the banker blurted, "You could get pregnant any minute and therefore be out of a job or quit one." At the same time I was also applying to graduate school again, this time in the field of psychology. It was here that I was confronted by the interviewing professor about the seductive and hysterical ways of women. He noted (perhaps he confabulated this) that in one of the letters of reference, the professor was quoted as saying I should stay home and be a wife and mother.

Discrimination continued. In 1974, I did indeed graduate with a master's in clinical psychology and was working the entire time of study. However, at my job, I was told I would not get a raise or promotion because "Tom, the man, has a family and he needs it more." Ironically, for the man, having kids was an asset to his earning potential. For the woman it was a detriment. As I begin to count the numerous and abiding discriminations and obstacles, even I am astounded at how blatant and entrenched prejudice against women was (and is).

Of course, I, like many women, wanted a balanced professional and family life. However, when I began to try to have children, my body was not cooperating. In the midst of grieving several miscarriages, in 1976, I was questioned in a job interview whether I planned to get pregnant again and then just up and leave them. At the time, I had doubts I would ever have children, so this was, as the cliché goes, like putting salt on a wound. (Well, as it turns out, the supervisor himself was fired later in this methadone clinic for his covert sociopathic behavior.)

It was not until I had a female supervisor at yet another mental health clinic that I could work without the hindrance of being objectified as a woman, of being treated as a seductive wench or as a bloody (literally) baby machine that would gum up the work schedule.

And before and during the time of my attempting to get pregnant, what were the obstetrician-gynecologists like? Well some were chauvinist and misogynous! As a graduate student in clinical psychology, I was seeing a psychiatrist for therapy myself. This lovely, but chain-smoking, to the detriment of her health, woman referred me to a male gynecologist who treated me with condescension and disdain. After a few uncomfortable encounters with him, I found care at Planned Parenthood that was without judgment and condescension.

Later, however, I did seek an obstetrician at a local women's hospital when I was having difficulty getting pregnant. I remember stealthily reading the letter of the urologist to the obstetrician intimating that because my husband had a below average sperm count, my miscarriages were probably not due to intercourse with him. I seethed but didn't say anything when the ob-gyn walked into the examining room, because that would have meant I read my own records. Not a popular concept at that time. Years later when I finally did give birth to my daughter, I again surreptitiously read my records. I had had a very difficult labor followed by a Cesarean delivery. Apparently, the surgeon nicked my bladder. They didn't bother to tell me, but I did know that the nurse in the hospital kept asking how well I was voiding. "Are you okay?" they would ask. Hmmm. Let's keep the little woman in the dark as to what really occurred.

Women were so isolated in what they were experiencing then. I had no desire to burn my bra, but I did want to be seen and heard. Growing up in the 1940's to the 1970's was a crazy-making experience. On the one hand, as a female I felt that things were changing; on the other hand, change did not go far enough. Yes, a woman could go to school, could get a job, but always with the qualifiers—the disability of gender.

It has been a struggle for many women to bear the weight of such a skewed world view. It may be compared to being aware of a seismic shift, an earthquake rumbling all around you, and noting that while this is occurring there are those around you who are unconscious, oblivious of the movements afoot. Yesterday as I felt the tremor, I questioned what was occurring, quickly deciding it was an earthquake. However, when I stepped out of the room where I had been sitting, there were several people walking in the corridor who were totally unaware of the occurrence. For a moment, I thought "okay, am I going crazy or what?" I had a reference point: there was an elderly woman I was talking to in her room that also felt the quake. Dementia aside, this woman was a bellwether of pertinent information. But the people in the hall were not. And the confirmation? The staff in the nurse's station were also shaken.

What an allegory for the experience of women and all those who have been oppressed in some way. We feel a seismic shift that something is changing yet there are those who are unconscious of any movement, of denying any movement.

Perhaps Mother Earth is truly grumbling at how not only women but the feminine principle has been so desecrated and maligned. Most assuredly, the planet has been desacralized for centuries. What if we took this seismic shift as an awaking of consciousness? Assumptive worlds to be shattered, the hand of the wounded feminine to arise from the broken asundered earth.

SEX CHANGE BY HYPNOSIS

I have had the opportunity to experience the hypnosis and gender work of Dr. Julie Linden. Through her experiential exercises, I was able to get in touch with the wounded feminine in myself. I do recall as a little child, maybe even as young as six, wondering what it would be like to be male. Maybe this was the wonderment I had after I had announced that I was going to be a priest, and was told promptly, "girls can't do that." My reaction prior to reflection was throwing myself on the sofa, crying and screaming. Maybe I even did some good Gestalt bodywork, kicking too. After that, I don't recall thinking about being a male until puberty, wondering with all the many changes occurring would I spontaneously become male instead of a burgeoning woman. Linden's guided imagery takes me back to the pondering—"what would be different if my sex changed?" She asked the group in guided imagery to further question, "What would I miss most of all of my own sex? What would be the benefit of my new sex? Is there an age associated with the change?" She delves deeper: "If my children change their sex, what would I miss, what would I gain?" And then, "If my favorite mentor were now of the opposite sex, how would that change my experience of that person?"

My response to this exercise was profound. I put myself back into my twenties as a male. What a difference that would have made. I would not have experienced sexual harassment from employers and professors. I would not have been demeaned as being "seductive" just by showing up. I would not have been passed over for job promotions or discriminated against for employment or a mortgage. Why, even male physicians would have listened to me and not sloughed me off as some hysterical female or, worse, sexually molested me under the guise of an internal exam. Unattractive (this is societally, culturally dependent) women are objects of disdain; attractive (also societally and culturally dependent) women are objects of prurient desire. I think over the years I've managed to fall into both categories depending upon age and weight, ten-year-old bespectacled chubby kid derisively called fatty bumps, non-dating teenager hidden in loose clothing, or a suddenly seen twenty-something.

I imagined too, that, as a man, I would feel safe walking down the street at night or walking into a parking garage any time of day. Unless a man goes through Linden's guided imagery of sex change, he may not get how savvy (and not naive) women are who are vigilant, perhaps even hyper-vigilant, in situations that seem almost innocuous to men.

One of my most significant mentors in graduate school was Paulina McCullough, a family therapist. To the guided imagery of changing her sex, I thought, ah, she would not have been mugged in the Psychiatric Institute Parking Garage if she had been a man. One less trauma in her life too. It should be noted that statistics, across the lifespan, indicate that women experience violence at a much higher rate than men. (See theduluthmodel.org, website of the Duluth Model of Domestic Abuse Intervention Programs.)

But perhaps there is some little reward for a woman's need for vigilance. Recently, I was invited to do crisis counseling at a bank that had been robbed the day before. As I met with staff, I observed something unexpected. I met with the teller who had been directly approached by the robber, and he told me his story; I talked with the other staff. Some of the office men who were not tellers did not appear to have noticed anything going on at first. And "hey, I am fine" was the attitude, and, "I wasn't afraid!" The teller also said he was "good." The employees seemed most concerned about the head teller's reaction. They described how upset she had been. I waited until she arrived to listen to her story also. What I discovered was that she, in her vigilance, had been the most aware.

It was she who noticed the robber as soon as he entered the bank, and she remarked how she was already on alert because of how he had behaved. And so she engaged the panic button instantaneously when she saw the robbery was about to occur. Yes, she was upset and shaken by the incident, but she was also the most observant and perceptive of any of the employees including the teller that was approached directly!

She described how she had surveyed the situation as soon as she felt something was amiss with the "customer." She noted who was in the lobby area—the employees, the customers; she took mental notes of who was behind the Plexiglas. In her keen observation, she had taken in the most information and perhaps was the most effective. Her vulnerability and emotional response was the result not of weakness but of courage. She epitomizes the rise of the wounded feminine (principle). She made empathic connection with all the people in her building and surveyed the situation based on compassion. She did not "do macho" but performed the right protocol. Yes, her cohorts might consider her weak because she cried. "She cried like a girl" would be a macho mantra. (Ever been to a social or sports activity and hear a father admonish his little boy for crying? I have. "Don't be a girl." says the manly man.) Her tears were at least perhaps out of relief that people in her care were safe. In her feminine vigilance, a wise vulnerability, she "saw more" than her colleagues had. Alertness and awareness are far greater assets than toughness, and might not fearlessness sometimes be a euphemism for clueless?

An incident in my own life while I was dating my husband may be another example of women versus men under threat. Anecdotes are never proof but they may at least spark reflection. In this case my future husband came from Boston to meet me in Washington DC for one of the major peace marches of 1969. I had arrived the day before with a car load of graduate student colleagues from the University of Dayton. After a long day of marching in the cold, my then boyfriend Larry and I walked to a restaurant for dinner. While we were eating, events outside took a turbulent turn. People were being tear-gassed and pushed back into the Mall area. We were unaware of all this. As we left the restaurant, at least six policemen walked abreast towards us.

Their intention was to sweep the streets and push all protesters into one area. I could feel the tension rising in my big strong man next to me. I didn't know what he was about to say or do but I intuitively piped up, sweetly stating, "but officers we're going back to our busses down the street, please let us through." False, that we were going to any busses, but true that we were not about to cause any ruckus. And true also that my wool six penny button coat and fluffy hat hardly rendered me a hardcore hippie, so I was believed. The officers allowed us to go on our way, away from the troubles that would ensue. (Perhaps my husband has a different rendition of the story but I stick to mine.)

The point is that anger or any aggressive words would not have worked in that situation., and fortunately it was one of those moments where I listened to my own wisdom of heart. And there is more. Perhaps it was because the night before I had participated in the candle light vigil walk (without Larry) in which we protesters went single file holding lit candles as we traversed the White House. I remember meeting eye to eye with a kind policeman who was part of the contingent that were protecting us from hecklers. He looked at me and said, "I wish I could walk with you." I responded, "I wish you could too." Often I think back to that moment and would have liked to instead have said "I thank you for where you are. You are part of this." So perhaps this brief encounter of kindness between a peace marcher and a policeman allowed me to be openhearted with that band of blue before me the next day.

Tina Fey, in her autobiography, *Bossy Pants*, attests to the need for gentleness in her TV show, *Thirty Rock*. She notes how she does not hire aggressive male scriptwriters. In other words, she screens out the bullies.

Kindness and connection stretches far ... and we need more of it.

Our Collective Experience of the Wounded Feminine

September of 2011 witnessed both the devastation in the aftermath of floods in New Jersey, New England, and New York (not to mention storms brewing in the South) and the tenth anniversary of September 11, 2001. September 11, 2001 was, as people attest to again and again, a terrible moment in our nation's history. This momentous tragedy struck the US and the world in ways well beyond the assassination of JFK. Perhaps more like the turbulence of World War Two in its psychological immensity.

Memories may be tricksters, but they may also carry our story: our history, or herstory. What I remember on that fate filled day is that after my office manager related a news bulletin she heard in her car, we turned on the TV. As we held each other taking in the surreal reality of it all, my knees buckled and I shook. In those first 24 hours I would have allowed any amount of military police state to take effect just to quell my fear, and calm my shaking body. Our son was an undergraduate at Georgetown University at the time. Washington was traumatized and in lockdown. Georgetown had lost faculty who had been passengers on the plane that flew into the Pentagon. Our daughter was in Boston at Harvard and the medical school was receiving bomb threats. I was overwhelmed with fear for my children. My body—brain was in hyper-drive—surely my amygdala and hippocampus were working hard maintaining my fear state. And my thinking mind was controlled by that fear. Hate rising toward the enemy, rage at whatever other was the cause.

Then, I caught myself. A voice came through saying, "Whoa, do you hear what you're saying and how you are thinking?" Vengeance, revenge, police state, ya-da-ya. Are you serious? The voice asked. Yes, I was serious all right. Listening to this voice deep within I became more afraid of who I was becoming. I began to settle myself down, choosing as best I could to face this horror with whatever equanimity and compassion I could muster and breathe more deeply.

Fortunately, I was in the midst of friends and colleagues who were likewise wanting to override fear and retaliation with centeredness and compassion. We held a candlelight vigil for those who had died or were lost. We created a peace chant together and taped it. (Our technology has evolved immensely in a decade. Our awareness needs to also!) I played that repeatedly in my office for months just so that I could maintain my balance and help my clients to do likewise.

A year later on the anniversary of 9/11, I was called to do some crisis intervention work at a finance firm local to my Pennsylvania office. This firm's site in New York was in proximity to the World Trade Center, and although no one in the office near me was in New York that day, the concern was that personnel might need support on the first year anniversary. Anniversaries of trauma and grief, especially the first year, can evoke a greater intensity of feeling. I expected this, but I did not expect the way it appeared that some employees still seemed stuck in the fear state that I had experienced for only the first day or two the year before. They were subsumed by fear and hyper vigilance. And I would presume they also felt strongly the need for vengeance.

Now, I didn't question these particular employees as to what news and TV programs they watch but my hunch is that their fear state was reinforced by what ever media outlets they were turning to. They seemed embedded in the same thinking I was accosted with early on: an us against them hyper-vigilance that was trapping them in post-traumatic stress. These were not employees who suffered direct traumatic loss. No friend or family member was involved or had died. Nevertheless, their subjective experience seemed profound. They carried a collective fear.

So what does this have to do with this book, this topic of *Quiet Wisdom in Loud Times: The Rise of the Wounded Feminine*. It is my sense that if our nation had been able to respond to that attack on 9/11 with less aggression and more compassion, had not gone hell-bent out of a collective fear but had instead met the global community with receptivity and compassion to the compassion shown us in the aftermath, that two wars could have been averted. Okay again, what's this got to do with the wounded feminine? It has to do with developing within the collective psyche a place for what is modeled by wisdom and the heart of compassion.

We went headlong and unbalanced into a violent thrust into the world. In that sense we shared the same lack of balance with the feminine as did—and does—the Taliban and Al Qaeda manifest.

Beyond the horror and the mayhem, and the people who directly suffered such dramatic loss of 9/11, I also saw two patriarchal worlds collide. The phallic twin Towers standing tall for money and power collapsing to the force and thrust of jets run violently amok by men who devalued and demeaned women while looking forward to eternal life with virgins.

What if our need to defend was tempered by a call to a quieter wisdom? What if, in that window of opportunity, when the world was holding us in our own goodness we would have allowed ourselves to be metaphorically soothed by such global embrace?

At that time, the world supported us, the US. Eva, the young woman who had been our exchange student from Hungary, contacted us, sending us love from her and her family. Friends from Canada phoned their support. Global compassion and care was palpable. Ah, the rise of the wounded feminine from the rubble of phallic towers destroyed by misguided men of a rigid patriarchal ideology using powerful phallic planes. Patriarchal power versus patriarchal power from which arose the Phoenix of the feminine principle: global cooperation and compassion was apparent. For a while, the US, in its collective trauma and grief met the kindness shown with an open heart. The wounded feminine principle was unfolding.

Unfortunately, the feminine principle was once again shut down; instead of maintaining the open hearts and connection that was felt globally, the US chose the vengeful, rageful tactics of the wounded, narcissistic patriarch. We initiated not one but two unending wars. Some might claim that our incursion into Afghanistan was necessary to "catch" the masterminds of the plot against America, particularly Osama bin Laden. The result, as we all know, was a protracted war in which we killed and maimed thousands of innocent civilians and captured and tortured many. Guantanamo, Cuba, remains an ignominy among many.

Under false pretenses our President George Bush began another war with Iraq. Again more mass destruction and more maiming and killing of hundreds of thousands of civilians. We don't do body counts of the so-called enemy — only of our soldiers: several thousand soldiers have died but many more are physically and emotionally wounded.

So thrusting forth with two wars post-9/11, we have hardly given heed to the wounded feminine rising. It has been more dirt on her grave; but she will not die!

If we begin to unearth her we might have a different view of our own PTSD in the wake of 9/11. I recall that after 9/11, I considered being a Red Cross mental health volunteer in New York. That never came to fruition because my practice became inundated with people who had anxiety and depression. They did not connect their issues with 9/11 but it was as though 9/11 became the tipping point of their emotional container: 9/11 precipitated the generalized crisis of confidence in their lives. A year later, the swell subsided and the people who had chosen to come, felt grounded again and those who didn't perhaps kept their emotional containers under lock and key once again.

Think of it, these are people for whom no one died in the towers or on the planes and who lived one hundred miles from New York City. This is evidence, I believe, that we reverberate profoundly with collective trauma. So if we were in tune with the feminine principle, wouldn't the corollary to this be that, if we suffered so from 9/11, we would see how much more have the people suffered—and are suffering—in Afghanistan, Iraq, Somalia and elsewhere?

Those who have lost loved ones in 9/11 no doubt have suffered traumatic grief. But what we, if we carry the feminine principle, realize is that they are not alone in their grief. That there is suffering that we as the US, have incurred on others that is , dare I say it, even worse. When the US gets enraged, watch out. (We are the ones who dropped the atom bombs on Japan not once but twice. Not only Hiroshima but just to get our point across on Nagasaki too.)

When we stop burying the feminine principle alive, we stop being the Bully.

May we some day heed this part of the bible: "She speaks her mouth with wisdom, and the teaching of kindness is on her lips. (*Proverbs 31:10—14*)

AN AFRICAN TALE OF WISDOM AND THE WOUNDED FEMININE

Jungian Analyst and author Thomas Moore says that "it is

better to spend a day meditating on a single page of Helen M. Luke's writing than to read a stack of books for enlightenment." My re-reading Helen Luke's telling of the African tale passed on to her from Laurens van der Post attests to Thomas Moore's insight. May this not be a "whisper down the lane" retelling of the story as I relate it to you. A Zulu wise man recounted it to Laurens van der Post who then retold it "as an offering of gratitude and respect to the women of the world." (Luke, p. 97)

In a certain African village a clique of young women set out to humiliate another young woman of the village. While they were jealous of her because she had a bead necklace that they perceived more beautiful than theirs, they also rejected her because she was "different."

Running down to the banks of the river, they planned to trap this "different" young woman. When she arrived alone, the group told her they had cast their necklaces into the river as an offering to the river god. Being of generous heart, the young woman tossed her necklace into the river as well. Then the others dug up their necklaces which they had buried in the sand, sneering and jeering, laughing at the young woman.

Now left alone again, bereft, she prayed to the god to restore what she had lost. She had been both well-meaning and foolhardy into having been so duped. As she wandered along the river bank praying, she heard a voice at last. "Plunge into a deep pool nearby," said the voice. Knowing this to be the voice of a god, without hesitation she plunged into the deep unknown—she made it all the way down to the river bed where an old woman sat. Ugly, repulsive even, was this old one. Covered with open sores, the old one beckoned to the girl, "Lick my sores."

Out of the depths of her compassionate heart, the young woman did so! She licked the repulsive sores. "Ah, because you have licked my sores without holding back, I will protect you and hide you when the demon comes. He devours the flesh of young women." At that moment, there was a roar and a gigantic male monster appeared, calling out that he smelled maiden there. The old woman, however, kept her word and the young woman was safely hidden. The monster boomed off, cursing and running.

Turning to the young woman, the old woman said, "Here is your necklace." But she placed upon her beads more beautiful than she had ever had before. She was then told to return to the village, but was also told, "When you have gone a few yards from the pool, you will see a stone in the path. Pick up this rock and throw it back into the pool. Do not look back; take up your ordinary life." The young woman did exactly as she was told.

When she got back to the village, the other girls, of course, noticed the beautiful necklace and wanted to know where it came from. She told them she had gotten it from the old woman on the river's bottom. They rushed down straight to the river's edge and dove in. And they too met the old woman. They too were asked to lick her sores. But they did not comply; instead they laughed at her—they would do no such thing—to lick sores so repulsive. Ugh! They demanded to have their own beautiful necklaces, nonetheless. In their clamoring, came the demon monster. These girls received no protection from the old woman and so, one after another, they were devoured.

Helen Luke informs us that the images contained in the story are "symbols of certain attitudes, conscious or unconscious, that are alive in each one of us and influence us in often un-realized and subtle ways. Stories like this are not manufactured by the intellect; they are the symbolic dreams of humanity." (p. 99)

Helen Luke's insights about this story couldn't be more apt than in contemporary culture. She points out that the necklace in Africa is a highly prized symbol of woman's identity and her worth as a person. Given that it concerns devotion to a divine, transpersonal value, the group of young women in the story play a particularly mean-spirited and unkind trick. What we see is group think, mass mentality "which so often covers and excuses hatred and cruelty. This is perhaps the worst menace in our society, requiring great effort and integrity to resist." (p. 99) Yet, just consider recent events in the news. The young man who jumped off a New York bridge, plunging to his death after his sex life was displayed on the internet by bullying college classmates. Bullying in schools, middle school on up, and in cyberspace, is rampant. "Don't be different, don't be other." We will make fun of you. The bullies also suffer group think.

Helen Luke warns us, however, about the young girl who takes the bait (p. 99):

This is surely a warning of the dangers that lie in wait for the

33

generous-hearted, who are so quickly induced by the slogans of some cause or crusade, fine in itself perhaps, and sponsored by people we long to please. We lose sight of our individual responsibility to reflect and to choose, and thus, as it were, we throw away our identity. Nevertheless, the story goes on to show us that such naïve enthusiasms, if they truly involve the intention of life itself, may indeed bring about the shock that leads us out of group thinking to the discovery of our meaning as individuals on a much deeper level.

The young girl, while having a rude awakening about her identification with her peers, does not wallow in resentment or remorse. She patiently remains in her solitude, staying alone beside the river of life, "praying that she might re-discover her value as a person, waiting for an inner voice to bring her wisdom" (p. 100). Not by striving upward (Climbing the ladder of success, perhaps?), but by delving into the deep can she find herself (p. 100):

She must plunge into the river of life unconditionally, risking mistakes or failure, not just throwing things, however valuable, into the river. Only by trusting herself to the unknown, both in her outer life and in her own hidden depths, would she find her unique way.

It's about surrender to the true, deep honest voice within; not to opinions, or convention, or ten-second sound bites. This is what we all need to hear. As we will see in a later chapter, Lisbeth Salander, heroine of the Larsson trilogy, certainly seemed to follow this wise counsel.

Plunging into the river of life is not bathing in a hot tub or wishing for the Fountain of Youth. Quite the opposite, in fact, for it is here we are "face to face with the ugliness, the suffering from which we have perhaps been protected hitherto in many ways" (p. 100). This, Helen Luke notes, is where the story provides its specifically feminine wisdom.

The old woman may symbolize the suffering that all women through the ages have undergone due to the contempt for feminine values. And yes this contempt is wrought by women as well as men.

(I have my therapy stories I can tell where mothers have shown contempt to daughters while their sons were held in high esteem. Or consider the negative animus—the mother of the ballerina in the *Black Swan* movie—more on this later.)

Secondly, on an individual, personal level, the old woman can represent that which we most despise in our own psyches. That part of us that repels us and from which we turn away in disgust.

Why paraphrase Helen Luke? Let me directly quote her here instead (Luke, p. 100-101):

The old woman's invitation is clear. 'You can't bring help to me by any kind of technical, scientific, impersonal and collective panacea, or by talk about justice and freedom. Only with your own saliva can you bring healing to these sores in yourself and in the world.' Saliva is symbolically a healing water that we are all born with. The licking of an animal is its one means of healing wounds, and we may remember Christ's saliva on the blind man's eyes. So the girl is asked to give of her own unique essence—to bring healing to the sores, not by words out of her mouth but by water from her mouth. Because she is on the threshold of true womanhood the girl at once responds out of that essential core of the feminine being—the compassionate heart. Her I would emphasize that true compassion bears no resemblance to a vague and sentimental pity. Compassion is not just an emotion; it is an austere thing and a highly differentiated quality of soul.

Luke sounds out the alarm: The universal threat that can so easily devour our womanhood is the demon of inferior masculinity. I think that what Luke refers to here is the negative animus driven by power and greed. To be lost in an imitation of men is to kill off the creative masculine, i.e., positive animus. Yes, this type of woman can be mightily successful, but she has sold her soul. A high price to pay for fleeting glory in a masculine world not balanced by the feminine principle.

The young woman in the African story makes no devilish bargain. She has no truck with greed and ambition but has the courage and the humility to lick the old woman's sores. And, Luke entertains, that it is at this precise moment that she receives her own individual and unique necklace, which is hers alone. This is truly differentiating because she is not simply taking back the old one that came from her family before her individuation into her own life. In family systems terms, we can say that the young woman is differentiating from her family of origin story and is individuating, differentiating.

However, she does not stay in the deep, but returns to ordinary life of the village. As Buddhists say, What does one do before Enlightenment? Chop wood, carry water. What does one do after Enlightenment? Chop wood, carry water. But with, ah, such presence and awareness. In our time, the young woman may raise a family or choose another profession, working outside the home. Or may do both. Yet Luke reminds us: "Whether she marries and bears children or not, this ancient responsibility of woman remains. She is the guardian of the values of feeling in her environment, and if she remains aware of that compassion, that quiet, hidden nurturing that is the center of her feminine nature, then her skills in any kind of work whatsoever will grow in the manner of trees, well-rooted and strong, and her creative spirit will be free. ... Always she will remember to 'lick the sores' and to remain still and hidden when the demon of greedy ambition threatens whether at home or in the public arena."

Quite frankly, I think Hillary Clinton several times in her career has "licked the sores" and has taken the high road of the positive animus woman. After President Obama won the nomination, she didn't turn bitter and resentful, but instead redoubled her efforts to be on his team. She collaborated! Assuredly, there may have been some backroom schmoozing. Nevertheless, I believe that Clinton acted out of positive animus with grace and dignity and that Obama did likewise. (I do believe he more than many of our presidents conveys the positive anima within.)

The same friend of my daughter who wondered about the rise of fundamentalism works in the state department. As she could give an eyewitness account of the feminine principle embodied in a stateswoman, I asked her "What is Secretary of State Clinton like?" She noted how caring and compassionate, brilliant and energetic she is.

Luke asks us to ponder the stone. She notes that the stone in all cultures is the symbol of the immortal Self. Therefore, throwing it back is honoring the sacredness, the divine that is of the river. In Hawaii, on the Big Island, where the goddess Pele, the volcano fire goddess, resides, it is said not to take the lava stone and put it in your pocket. Throw it back—give it back to the goddess. There are many stories where people have taken the lava home only to later send it back to the island claiming bad luck. Other travel writers dispute the stories and pooh-pooh the concern. Having been to Pele's volcano twice, I can safely say I left the lava rocks where they were. I think whether or not "things happen" it's wise to note that there is indeed an honoring of the sacred—it would be like going into a grand cathedral and stealing a shard of stained glass or chipping at the stone, just to have a piece.

So what do the young women who didn't care to awaken to the meaning of life, but instead went willy nilly as a mob? Their contemporaries would be searching for outward success; their own power or for powerful men, wealth, publicity, perhaps even grasping for peak, spiritual experiences. Luke enjoins us to see that these women "refused with contempt the essential task of a woman, the compassionate 'licking the sores' in themselves and in their immediate environment." (Pg. 102) Perhaps devoured by the demon of patriarchy? This is actually a task for us all, both men and women, to face that which we avoid—the darkness, the despair, the suffering of the world—we all need to lick these sores with compassion not only to heal our own wounded feminine principle but to heal the world as well.

In the next chapter, we will set out to define patriarchy and other terms that will help understand better why the "rise of the wounded feminine" must continue to occur.

2

COMING TO TERMS
WITH TERMS

*The opposite of love is not hate, it's indifference....the opposite
of life is not death, it's indifference. (Elie Wiesel)*

What a very masculine chapter heading for a book about
the wounded feminine principle. Would that the definitions
of patriarchy, *anima*, and *animus*, and complex and archetype, be without nuance and ambiguity. However, black and
white, all or nothing, nicely logical and straightforward they
are not.

I feel like a Fraggle (the little creatures of the HBO series,
Fraggle Rock), who goes to the Trash Heap—the Fraggle's
goddess of wisdom—everytime I genuflect to this ubiquitous and anonymous source of knowledge calling itself
Wikipedia. Wikipedia defines patriarchy as a social system
where the male is the primary authority figure. Thus, the

men are central to social organization, and fathers/husbands hold authority over women, children, and property. "Within feminist theory, patriarchy refers to the structure of modern cultural and political systems, which are ruled by men. Such systems are said to be detrimental to the rights of women. However, ... as patriarchal systems of government do not benefit all men of all classes." (Wikipedia, 2011)

I would go beyond the "Wikipedian" definition of patriarchy and see it in the broader psychological sense of oppression of the feminine principle for both men and women, that denigration of the feminine goes beyond gender.

Fr. Richard Rohr, a noted author and director of the Center for Action and Contemplation (cacradicalgrace.org), gives an online daily spiritual reflection. On September 8, 2010, he says:

> *One of the reasons women have become so angry at men is that they're tired of being manipulated, objectified, and devalued. In fact, all of Western civilization is tired of the feminine being devalued. It's tired of the rational "command-and- control" model for reality. For far too long, the negative masculine energy has been running everything.*

It is refreshing to hear a clergyman (yes, <u>man</u>) articulate the importance of the feminine principle in both men and women—in all things, in fact. He implores men to do their spiritual work so that the positive meaning of the masculine can be found. And, as I stated earlier, this is not about gender. The feminine principle manifests with some men better than in some women.

Another clergyman, Father Thomas Berry, the noted spiritual ecologist, defined in his book *Dream of the Earth* that "patriarchy has now been brought forward as a way of indicating the larger sources of responsibility for what is happening not only with women, but also with the total civilizational structure of our society and even with the planet itself. The sense of *patriarch* has now evolved as the archetypal pattern of oppressive governance by men with little regard for the well-being or personal fulfillment of women, for the more significant human values, or for the destiny of the earth itself." (p. 143)

In 1995, I attended a Common Boundary conference where I heard Thomas Berry speak. While I listened to him, a thought came to me about patriarchy—as patriarchy breaks down, perhaps it wants to take the feminine earth with it. I considered that perhaps an individual man feels impotent in this lost patriarchy, can't find his entitlement, and so rages against a woman, leading to rape. He is losing his power and so makes a show of brute force, not seeing his connection and not recognizing his own feminine within. (As I write, military men are being convicted of rape crimes against military women. Are these men so threatened by their cohorts that they violently rape them?) And also the collective patriarchy rages against the breakdown and collectively rapes Mother Earth, another show of brute force.

Patriarchy does not recognize the connection of feminine and masculine humanity and earth. Thomas Berry himself talked about a deep hidden rage against the human condition and noted that we need to have a shared dream. The patriarchal stance is out of balance and prescribes to hierarchical power and domination, rather than collaboration and compassion.

Riane Eisler, authored *Sacred Pleasure*, as well as *The Chalice and the Blade*. She reminds us in *Sacred Pleasure* that the terms *feminine* and *masculine* are constructs of our language that are part and parcel of our dominator society. In the dominator society, "masculinity is equated with dominance and conquest, and femininity with passivity and submissiveness." This is not about gender, *per se*. With that caveat in mind, we may view her table of the Dominator Model versus the Partnership Model, as adapted by Jungian analyst David Richo, in his book, *Mary Within*:

David Richo, based on Riane Eisler's work, gives us this table:

Component	Dominator Model	Partnership Model
Gender relations	Males ranked higher than females	Males and females of equal rank and feminine qualities are honored
Violence	Violence is institutionalized, e.g., capital punishment, war	Accent on nonviolent resolution of conflict
Social structure	Hierarchical and authoritarian; values killing and exploiting	Egalitarian; values giving birth and nurturing

Sexuality	Coercion, eroticization of dominance, and procreation as main purpose of sex	Accent on bonding with freedom of choice and mutual pleasure
Religion	Dogma over nature, patriarchal authority, retaliatory God and afterlife as reward/punishment	Divine as unconditional love, moral accent on empathy rather than obedience
Pleasure/ Pain	Pain as sacred, submission as the price of pleasure	Pleasure within a loving bond is sacred as is caring and freedom
Power and Love	Power is for control of others and love justifies abuse	Highest power is to love and share light of consciousness

What becomes evident in comparing the dominator, or patriarchal, model to the partnership model, is that what is deemed stereotypically *masculine* outranks that which is stereotypically deemed *feminine* in the dominator society. There is no equality, or balance, between the masculine and the feminine.

Furthermore, in the Dominator Model, violence and abuse is institutionalized. (I would say that bullying is a form of institutionalized violence. We expect our children not to bully, yet we set poor examples both in the home and on the national scene.)

Richo succinctly states, "The dominator model focuses on a superior-inferior dualism, a sharply divided submission-dominance style in human relating. In the part-nership model the focus is on actualization of one's power for good, not success at being in control. Partnership is about affiliation and interconnectedness, not competition; creation, not destruction; relationship, not hierarchy. It seeks to transform conflict, to dissolve it by nonviolence and compassion instead of violence and retaliation."

To move from the superior-inferior dualism of patriarchy, a consideration of the Jungian concepts of *anima* and *animus* may help.

As awkward as discussion of *anima, animus,* and patriarchy and feminine principle may be, I don't think there are better concepts to help define a 21st Century situation where the powers that be, the patriarchy, won't let go enough to share the reins with the feminine principle that would bring the out-of-control horses carrying our worldly wagon of woes onto a more enlightened and less precipitous path.

ANIMA, ANIMUS, AND THE FEMININE PRINCIPLE

Emma Jung may look to be a lightweight in the movie, A Dangerous Method; and, as C.G. Jung's forbearing (and forever child-bearing) wife, she did not stop him from his affair with the formidable and brilliant Sabina Spielrein. So perhaps Emma may be mistaken for a collapsed woman, a woman who yields to the patriarchy. However, she and Spielrein both may have been as much progenitors as they were midwives of C.G. Jung's creative theories.

The concepts of anima and animus are not easy to hold. They slip and slide from unconsciousness to consciousness. Then when we are conscious of them, because they are of soul quality (*anima,* in Latin meaning feminine soul, and

46

animus, referring to masculine soul), they are both spiritual and ephemeral. The character Sabina Spielrein asks C.G. Jung in the film *A Dangerous Method*, "Don't you think there's something male in every woman and something female in every man?" (40:38).

Early in the twentieth century, Emma Jung wrote on the topics of *animus* and *anima*. We may question, given the Victorian times in which all of these Jungians lived, whether or not the notions of *animus* and *anima* are antiquated or obsolete today. They are not.

When I read Emma Jung, her words reverberate, resonating within me. In writing of the woman's *animus*, she notes (p. 38):

> *The attitude demanded here—which is, to do something for its own sake and not for the sake of another human being—runs counter to feminine nature and can be achieved only with effort. But this attitude is just what is important, because otherwise the demands that is part of the nature of the anima is, and therefore justify itself in other ways, making claims which are not only inappropriate ..., but which produced precisely the wrong effects.*

I think what Emma Jung points to here is the burning need for a woman to own her own contra-sexual masculine soul and use it to thrust forward into her own individuating journey—not for the sake of another man nor for the sake of continuing the patriarchy. It is about a woman working on her journey to wholeness that necessitates her honoring her masculine within. If she dismisses the masculine as a necessary part of herself, she may never find her own voice or her own authority, continuing to question her thoughts and feelings, not allowing herself to be authentic. If she takes on the contra-sexual as a way to collude with the negative masculine that is the shadowy underbelly where power and domination lie, then she also loses her own authority, becoming an unconscious daughter of the patriarchy.

Hence, if a woman is overtaken by the animus drive within, she may align herself with logic (or power) to the detriment of relationship. That is, she dismisses the feminine principle to align with the masculine, and consequently with patriarchy's constricted focus. If a man dismisses the feminine principle by demeaning the anima within then he too colludes with the patriarchal imbalance.

My personal and professional experience attests to this deference to logic to the detriment of feeling. It wasn't until I re-read Emma Jung recently that I came to a better understanding of not only my client's relationship with her daughter but with my mother-daughter relationship as well.

My client had written a very logical letter to her daughter about how the girl's father was being irresponsible about money ever since the parents separated. The daughter reacted with emotion to this missive, berating her mother for once again speaking ill of her father. My client couldn't understand why her daughter couldn't get the facts of the situation. Forgetting Emma Jung's words, but not forgetting her message, I implored my client to see that the last thing her daughter needed in this fraught situation was logic and reason. She needed warmth and understanding from her mother.

Likewise, I too have had altercations with my daughter where I wanted her to see my logic about a situation, and in doing so I totally discounted her feelings about it. Fortunately, I had my own moment of truth and apologized for my negative animus-ridden behavior.

So Emma Jung's words I quote here may be last Century, but her message remains relevant (*Animus and Anima*, p. 22):

... in the field where the creative activity of woman flowers most characteristically, that is, in human relationships, the creative factor springs from feeling coupled with intuition or sensation, more than from mind in the sense of logos. Here, the animus can be actually dangerous, because it injects itself into the relationship in place of feeling, thus making relatedness difficult or impossible. It happens only too frequently that instead of understanding a situation—or another person—through feeling and acting accordingly, we think something about the situation or the person and offer an opinion in place of a human reaction. This may be quite correct, well-intentioned, and clever, but it has no effect, or the wrong effect, because it is right only in an objective factual way. Subjectively, humanly speaking, it is wrong because in that moment the partner, or the relationship, is best served not by discernment or objectivity but by sympathetic feeling. It very often happens that such an objective attitude is assumed by a woman in the belief that she is behaving admirably, but

the effect is to ruin the situation completely. The inability to realize that discernment, reasonableness, and objectivity are inappropriate in certain places is often astonishing. I can only explain this by the fact that women are accustomed to think of the masculine way as something in itself more valuable than the feminine way and superior to it. We believe a masculine objective attitude to be better in every case than a feminine and personal one. This is especially true of women who have already attained a certain level of consciousness and an appreciation of rational values.

A woman's relationship to her animus is a far different story than a man's relationship to his anima. Emma Jung contends that it is quite easy for a woman to obey the authority of the animus, and also the man, with "slavish servility." It would seem that the masculine control sense of patriarchal domination is so ingrained that both women and men have the unfortunate and peculiar proclivity to drink from the same toxic trough. Ah synchronicity: I am sitting at Longwood Gardens as I read about Emma Jung's words. As I look up, a young man grabs his girlfriend from behind, holding her back close to him as he wraps his arm around the front of her across her shoulders and neck. She laughingly, but uncomfortably, grasps his arms, attempting to politely pull him off. He eventually lets go. An innocuous encounter? Or again, just another behavioral example of how one man automatically and unconsciously thinks a woman is not only his pride but also his possession?

Women, then, have an opposite task of men when confronting the contra-sexual aspects of the self. Where men may need to face what they have unconsciously or consciously always considered inferior—that is the feminine—women must sometimes lift themselves up (by the bootstraps perhaps) to identify with the masculine, not as superior, but on the level of equality. Emma Jung notes her conversation with an American woman physician who decried how her women patients deprecated their own sex. And it continues. We see it today manifested in eating disorders as well as in domestic violence. If women do not give the feminine its due value, who will? Few men will dismiss their own sex. Emma Jung astutely observes that while many girls would gladly be men, nary a man would wish the reverse. Granted, there are those transgendered individuals that opt for this; but, for the general population of men and women, Emma Jung's observations still stand.

In fact her ideas correlate with Dr. Linden's hypnotic work, described in the previous chapter, when Dr. Linden guided us to imagine ourselves as the opposite sex.

It seemed empowering to me to imagine myself a man. The men who shared their experience did not appear comfortable with the sex change: it seemed to me to feel diminishing to them. So it is not surprising then that the man experiences the anima quite differently than the woman experiences the animus. "When a man discovers his anima and has to come to terms with it, he has to take up something which previously seemed inferior to him." The man encountering the feminine in himself may be outwardly quite egalitarian and even feminist. Nevertheless, the patriarchal stance is in our genes.

Our trauma history has become embedded all the way to the genetic level—carried in our biological inheritance. But we are not determined by it. Biology is not destiny; when we become conscious, we can heal our traumas and re-right, re-write our genes.

In my early years as a psychologist and family therapist, I had the good fortune to meet and learn from many pioneers of family therapy. Perhaps the grandfather of family therapy, Murray Bowen, and his theories captivated me the most. He did not just consider the individual, couple, or family in the session; he was interested in the inter-generational patterns in the family tree. He wanted to know who the great-grandparents, the grandparents, the parents were, both who was born and who died when and where. He derived emotional patterns in the facts of the family as they cascaded down the generations. Bowen intuited that there was a biological foundation in how the stresses, griefs, and traumas of one generation informed succeeding generations

Now, with the burgeoning field of epigenetics, Bowen's theories prove true. Epigenetics is the study of the influence of the environment upon the genome—the individual's DNA identity. No, your DNA doesn't change, but the environment does "tag" the various expressions of your genes, so that parts of your genome don't get expressed. Geneticists, such as Randy Jirtle. Use this analogy: consider genome (the particular DNA) of an individual to be like a computer, and the epigenome would be like the software (see the July 24, 2007, PBS *Nova* program regarding Epigenetics, *Ghost in Your Genes*).

So you can say, "Okay, big deal, I eat junk food or smoke cigarettes and debilitate my body. It's my body, so what?" Well, the problem is what you do to your body that changes the biochemical expression of a gene gets passed down the generations. What our grandparents did does affect us. But it is not only what we or our grandparents did themselves, it is also what has been done to them or us that is especially profound psychologically. If our grandparents suffered traumas—wars, violence, poverty—the emotional effects are transmitted not just behaviorally, but in the expression of genetics.

That is the downside. The upside is that this epigenetic effect on the genome can be changed. This is where choice and awareness come in. We actually can heal the past—at least the DNA expression of our history—through psychotherapy, learning about our family mythology and transcending its constrictions, learning how to emotionally regulate and defuse our emotional reactivity. Turns out our bodies are more than ourselves! We truly are connected to the past and we can change the future generations by changing ourselves now.

AND EMMA JUNG MIGHT AGREE

Emma Jung writes: "even though she may think otherwise consciously, the idea that what is masculine is in itself more viable than what is feminine is born in her blood. This does much to enhance the power of the animus. What we women have to overcome, in our relation to the animus is not pride but lack of self-confidence and the resistance of inertia."

As much as women have come into their own authority in many ways since Emma Jung wrote in the 1930's, to say that the feminine principle is fully acknowledged and that the *animus* of a woman and the *anima* of a man is truly lived out is like saying racism and prejudice is a thing of the past because we have elected a black president.

Indeed, that women have awakened to this power and have been finding their voice and that we have elected a black president is all the more reason that the patriarchal status quo would push against that movement into consciousness and wants to pull us again into a state of denial as well as of inequality—not only of individual persons with the emerging energetic change necessary for the rebalancing and re-centering of the collective consciousness.

To rebalance and re-center, a wedding needs to occur. Feeling, emotion, and loving connection need to be on par, seen as important as, rationality, logic, and objectivity. The feminine principle in general is dismissed as inferior. Hence, even women themselves denigrate it as "less than the man." (Later, we'll see how a feminine-principled man may feel guilty of his *anima* for betraying the old boy network.)

I remember as a child, feeling, quite clearly, the ambivalence of this state of affairs. I both wanted to succeed academically and professionally as a girl and later as a woman. However, I especially recall, even at the age of eleven or twelve, worried that girls don't ask for microscopes or chemistry sets. And, wow, my boy cousins and my brother and his friends are so much smarter than I. I held them in esteem for their facility with what looked to me to be a sense of confidence in their own self efficacy. Of course, the culture surrounding me never countered my ambivalence but imbued it with the confirmation of the status quo. Yes, girls were second-class even when they were first in class, honor roll and American Legion awards notwithstanding.

The tension we live here is not that women should eschew the feminine principle but that both men and women honor its presence and nurture its flowering as an antidote to the lopsided masculine dominated patriarchy that continues to burden us.

And come to think of it, flowers often represent the feminine principle. Yet in the struggle toward spring, have you ever seen the snowdrop or crocus push its way through the dead leaves left from autumn, emboldening itself with its own leaf as sword? Nothing stops its masculine thrust up from the Earth, daggering the debris in its way. So is this the metaphor for the masculine element, the *animus*, in a woman? Or for the feminine principle connection to masculine power? That strong surge toward light and life itself? But there is still much work ahead.

The diminishment of the feminine principle is noted by Emma Jung (*Animus and Anima*, p. 23):

Up to now in our world, the feminine principle, as compared to the masculine, has always stood for something inferior. We only begin at present to render it justice. Revealing expres-

In the midst of winter, the flower blossoms: a "sword" through old autumn
leaves. (*Photo by the author.*)

*sions are "only a girl" or "a boy doesn't do that," as is often
said to boys to suggest that their behavior is contemptible.
Then too, our laws show clearly how widely the concept of
woman's inferiority has prevailed.*

Emma Jung's observation that the feminine principle is considered inferior still holds. The "Revealing Expressions" she
notes can be heard today.

In fact, let me relate my recent experience with this.

Fathers, Sons, and the Feminine Principle

As I swim in my favorite oasis of summer, a pond replete with filter system and a beach, I overhear a child say, "Ouch, I skinned myself." Father retorts, "Oh, you're tough!" I let the comment go figuring that perhaps the Dad has assessed the situation accurately as "nothing to fret about." Awhile later, however, I hear the son say again something about how he is hurting, to which the father replies in a deep voice, "You're tough."

Now I begin to wonder if this is not a case where the father needed his inner feminine to come forward so that he could lead with his warmth (as a male psychologist-colleague would say to his male clients) and give his child an empathetic ear. Perhaps all this little boy needed was for his Dad to bend down and check his knee, give it a pat and a kiss. Instead, father ignored his child's pleas, and gave him no eye contact or the briefest of concerns.

Granted, this father may love his son dearly and may even think that his actions with him will harden him for the game of life. The father, I would guess, wants to make his son in his image—and his image of himself is more than likely that of a "man's man"—tough, invulnerable. Perhaps this is a man that bristles at showing any feeling other than anger. Vulnerability, then, would be a sign of weakness.

There is a Native American proverb that says "Gentleness is the greatest strength." This father would be even stronger, braver if he could show his son that it is okay to feel vulnerable sometimes, and that TLC (tender, loving care) is not just a "girl thing."

On another day at the Pond, I overheard another father remark to his son, "don't act like a girl." The message to be tough may be slightly less derogatory, but both messages convey the idea that to be vulnerable is to be feminine and that to be feminine is inferior.

What kind of world would it be if fathers could teach their sons gentleness and acceptance of the feminine principle within? Comments of "you're tough" and "don't act like a girl" are signs that the feminine is wounded within these men. What if the wounded feminine were allowed to rise in all its strength and power and be wounded no longer? The feminine principle that contains empathy and care united within the masculine would make a meek and mighty man; indeed, gentleness is the greatest strength.

DAVID BROOKS VS. DAVID ZIRIN

Clearly, David Brooks, the New York Times columnist, did not get the memo that "gentleness is the greatest strength" because soon after my experience at my swimming hole, he bemoaned in an article (July 5, 2012) that boys just were not allowed to be boys these days. Hamlet or Henry V would never have made it in our school system, he opines: "The education system has become culturally cohesive, rewarding and encouraging a certain sort of person: one who is nurturing, collaborative, disciplined, neat, studious, industrious, and ambitious." This is a problem? It sounds like a movement towards incorporating the feminine principle in schools, but for David Brokks it portends the end of the rebellious spirits of boys, all those would be Hamlets and Henry V's.

On the heels of Brooks' comments, and in counterpoint to them, David Zirin writes about Serena Williams and Title IX (See his July 9, 2012, blog at TheNation.com). When Serena Williams won her fifth Wimbledon (July 7, 2012), Zirin says she was asked the usual question of the female athlete, "was it difficult to control your emotions?" As a man who appears to embody the feminine principle, Zirin observes that women are considered "too emotional, too hysterical, too mercurial to be taken seriously in any walk of life. This runs so deeply in the marrow of US society, we rarely—when politicians are lobbying for involuntary vaginal ultrasounds—step back and comment on just how destructive it is."

Despite the fact that the US ranks seventy-eighth in the world in female legislative representations, and that women remain on tenterhooks regarding pay equity, health care, and reproductive freedom, Zirin takes heart in celebrating the fortieth anniversary of the passing of Title IX legislation which gave equal opportunity in sports and education to young women.

The Women's Sports Foundation notes that forty years ago only 1 in 35 girls played sports in high school. Now the ratio is 1 in 3.

I can attest to my own lack of opportunity in athletics. "Girls just didn't do that." I was "lucky" that I had ballet for a few years in grade school and until I could drive a bicycle to ride. My daughter, on the other hand, was named scholar athlete at her high school and continued in sports in college and now hikes and climbs. Even as a toddler, she was more active and mobile than her brother. He was the quiet observer of his older sister's love of anything athletic.

Ironically, however, Title IX did not help women coaches. In 1972, 90% of coaches of college women's athletic teams were women. Now it is 42%. As soon as schools had to treat women's sports seriously, men competed for the coaching positions.

Zirin refers to journalist Megan Greenwell, who says, "... once men started wanting jobs coaching women, men started getting a disproportionate number of those jobs. It's one of the most obvious, yet least talked-about, forms of institutional sexism out there: Coaching jobs are only for women where men don't want them."

Anecdotal outliers to the norm, perhaps, but if not, maybe they are more indications of the subtlety of the patriarchy in daily life: Two vignettes—one again about the pond, the other about a young woman in the workplace.

Aligning with Megan Greenwell's comments about male coaches being preferred over females, our swim club for seven years has tried to oust the female lifeguard and pool manager. Most members really liked Sophie. She was a great model of the balance of the masculine and feminine. A divorcée, she raised thee fine sons while teaching elementary school. In my observations, she did a superlative job of being mother hen, emergency nurse, organizer, disciplinarian, caretaker. Her staff respected her as she respected them. She could be tough; she could be kind. It seemed she was always there, in and out, making sure things were cleaned up morning and night. Lifeguards at off times were busy sweeping and raking. And when the guards were at their stations, they were attentive. There was a sense of feminine care. Yet Sophie brought laughter and fun with her too. So her staff stayed for years! Retention was extremely high.

Yet the powers that be decided that they could finally ease Sophie out and bring a man in. Despite the fact that most members liked Sophie's management style, the board found a way to show her the door. I believe that there were those (mainly men, but also a woman) who just didn't like having a feisty woman (who was not afraid to correct any member for an infraction) in charge. So finally the board got their wish. I will not argue that this man, also a teacher, is not a good, decent, competent person. However, things don't seem as well maintained and organized as they had been under Sophie's tenure. Yes, hopefully, this man will get the hang of things by next year. But Sophie had already had the place running smoothly. What's the old adage, if it ain't broke, don't fix it? Sophie's guards were seasoned, some were in college, some were teachers. The lineup of the new guards under this new tutelage are young and inexperienced and not as watchful as they need to be. They too will hopefully grow into their authority. But I still wonder that if Sophie were a male, would she still have her job?

The other story is about a young woman who was recommended for training by one of her supervisors. She was told by the man, "I am giving your name, along with Tom's, to Joe for this training—I am giving it to him in no particular order. Without conferring with her, Joe decides that Tom will get the training. Well, David Brooks, where is your Hamlet or Henry V now? This young woman considered the decision may have been based on gender and the old boy network was given preference.

Unlike how I was at her age, swallowing my anger and not finding my voice, this young woman spoke up and asked how the decision was made, questioning his rationale.

This young woman carries the feminine principle aligned with the positive animus and her behavior indicates an evolution of consciousness—she is moving out of the old frame, as is the man who had the following dream.

A FEMININE-PRINCIPLED MAN HAS A DREAM

A very gentle man who appears to accept his anima well nevertheless had the following dream. Keep in mind that a dream may have its relation to the dreamer's outer reality but it is also telling a story of the dreamer's unconscious and also touches the collective unconscious.

I HAVE KILLED THE OLD MAN OF THE HOUSE

I have murdered, purposely, the aging patriarch of the house I am in. I don't know how I've done it but I have. I killed him because he had been rigidly oppressing the woman of the house, his adult daughter who cared for him. I killed him to liberate her and to make an inheritance available. I know it was OK to do this because I saw the woman dutifully carrying him down the steps and pausing for a moment to consider dropping him over the railing, an act that would have killed him. She couldn't do it although at least part of her wanted to. So I then somehow, and without anyone else knowing it, killed him. No one including the daughter, another younger adult woman, and a younger male, all of whom live in the house, know that I did it (killed him) but they know he was killed.

Now an older, very experienced detective arrives at the house. He is determined to solve the mystery. I am scared and feel guilty but don't believe I've left any clues. We are in a big, square pool (50' x 50'). The police have emptied the water from it to assist the investigation. At the bottom of the pool is an extensive lining of either empty shells or empty seed husks. There is a large, round section in the center composed of what look like wet, empty, seed pods of a darker color. We are all in this emptied pool, the women, the younger man, the detective, and me. The detective, who looks like an older, be speckled [sic], mustached, tall, thin man wearing a hat, walks around looking very carefully for clues. He picks up some of the empty, wet seed husks form the bottom and looks at them carefully. I think it will be very difficult for him to find any evidence connecting me to the murder. Still, I feel scared.

Now I am back in the house. The police are inspecting both floors and still haven't found anything. In a separate room, the daughter of the old man begins to suggest that she believes, sadly, that I did it. We are interrupted and don't continue the conversation.

I now am outside, driving in my car away from the house. I see my younger male friend (blond, light beard, and in his mid 20's) riding a motorcycle and I pull alongside of him. He lets me know that he is concerned he will be blamed for the old man's death. We, shortly afterward, separate and go in different directions.

Throughout this dream I feel a strong sense of guilt and think about turning myself in. However, I realize I would make things worse and bring shame and heartache to my family and close friends. I know I have to go on without saying anything to anybody.

All dreams are multileveled, multifaceted. Multilayered. They can be interpreted in any number of ways and of course are dependent upon the dreamer's own psychological dynamics and life situations and contexts. However, the dreamer can also carry a message of the collective unconscious. For my purposes here, I consider that this dream can be viewed collectively, and relates to the dying patriarchy that the younger masculine must kill off and not provide life support for. It can also be interpreted here as the dreamer is facing his anima, his need to protect his own burgeoning feminine principle. Yet even he, enlightened as he is, still feels guilty for killing off the patriarch. He, after all, is a man, and as such is still part of the "old boy network." Actually, we all—men and women alike—are part of the patriarchal framework.

CHANGE AND CHANGE BACK

If ever I have experienced polarities of emotion simultaneously, it is now, in this mind-bending zeitgeist when new consciousness is being born—the wounded feminine is rising—as the patriarchy rattles sabers and shakes its fist at such phenomenal change. I am delighted to witness the wounded feminine rising, yet admit to feeling anger and anxiety at the "change-back maneuvers." The issue of contraception and the church is seeking center stage. As monumental as it was, I had not considered readily available contraception as a paradigm change until I read Sara Robinson. She makes the case that with contraception, for the first time in thousands of years, the biology of the woman was not destiny. For centuries, women prior to contraception, were controlled by, and were the property of, MEN.

Is contraception yet another Copernican Revolution? Copernicus showed that the earth (and <u>man</u>) was no longer the center of the universe. Suddenly truth: the earth revolved around the sun, rather than the other way around. A blow to collective egocentrism. Now with contraception, another blow to patriarchal control where men no longer have dominance, this time over women. However, not everyone is getting the message.

Robinson puts it as follows:

But perhaps most critically for us right now: mass-produced, affordable, reliable contraception has shredded the ages-old social contracts between men and women, and is forcing us all (willing or not) into wholesale re-negotiations on a raft of new ones.

And, frankly, while some men have embraced this new order— perhaps seeing in it the potential to open up some interesting new choices for them, too — a global majority is increasingly confused, enraged, and terrified by it. They never wanted to be at this table in the first place, and they're furious to even find themselves being forced to have this conversation at all.

The historical facts of the dominator culture that have existed for a few thousand years is known. That women and children were property of men is disturbingly wrong; that women and children still are the property of men in many places is beyond the pale. And now that we see the Catholic bishops, who have covered up sexual abuse crimes for years, rail against women and their reproductive rights; and we see male legislators who do likewise. These are both flagrant attempts at societal regression.

In 1995, Riane Eisler comments in *Sacred Pleasure* about how contraception, or lack thereof, has always been an issue of male domination. Control of women's reproductive rights keeps women in "their place." Eisler notes how powerful religious hierarchies remain silent about uncaring and violent sex, including genital mutilation and rape. (So then it is not surprising that in 2012, we see how many sexual abuse crimes were hushed!) Instead of utilizing resources to stop the violence, some religious leaders implore the victims not to use contraception or have abortions. "... Pope John Paul II's response to the mass rapes of women in Bosnia was not to back those who are today working to have mass rapes finally recognized as war crimes. Rather, it was to pray that the violated women not have abortions." (Eisler, p 314)

I do recall—1960?—I must have been 13 or 14—on the cover of the Jesuit Catholic weekly, *America* was an artist rendering in black-and-white of a woman staring at the reader, the headline next to her was something to the effect, "where will contraception—the birth control pill—take us?"

Interesting, although I was unconscious of the profundity of this question, I nevertheless took it so to heart that I pondered that cover for years. As I remember, the Catholic Church at the time wasn't quite sure how to handle the pill. It was up for discussion. This was ten years after the same church proclaimed the Assumption of Mary as infallible doctrine. (This, by the way, is one of only two "infallible" papal proclamations—the other was Mary's being born without original sin—so it was her "immaculate conception" when she was conceived. Any other pronouncements by any popes do not carry the import of "infallibility.")[1]

To non-Catholics, and particularly non-Christians, this may appear to be an arcane and inconsequential dogmatization about the obscure woman Mary who gave birth to the

1. In an attempt to document my adolescent memory, my family and I went on a wild romp through library stacks to find the cover in question. While we could not find the pen and ink drawing I recalled, we did find that there was an article about Dr. John Rock, fervent Catholic and Harvard gynecologist, who supported the use of "the pill" as an alternative to the rhythm method. This commentary did not support the physician's views; and, while the Catholic Church had not yet taken a definitive stand against "the pill" as a means of birth control, it was already becoming clear that the Catholic Dr. Rock was not converting the clergy to his enlightened view. Was the cover a figment of my imagination? That still remains elusive. While searching for the cover in question, we also perused every *Jubilee* magazine from 1958 to 1963. Although we did not find the black and white drawing I hoped for, we did discover a renewed interest in this magazine, which had a brief life in liberal Catholic thought from 1953 to 1967. It was heartening just to peruse the articles and reflections: stories about freedom marchers, medical mission sisters, writings by theologians such as Hans Küng and contemplatives such as Thomas Merton. What does it say that the Catholic journal that most reflected the feminine principle is now defunct? The mystery may remain unsolved regarding the woman of my memory, but there is no mystery as to how the *Jubilee* magazines of my youth kindled my care for the feminine principle.

historical Jesus. Actually, Carl Jung saw this as a monumental event. It meant that the feminine was finally raised in stature to the provenance of God and her son. Here again, the rise of the wounded feminine. The mother of the Pieta is recognized as being of such importance that her body too was raised from the dead. Finally, her matter (note to relation to mater) mattered.

Mary, Queen of Heaven, as depicted at Saccidananda Ashram, Tamil Nadu, India. *Photo by the author.*

C.G. Jung saw this as a great turn of consciousness regarding the feminine principle. And ten years later, birth control! Little did the hierarchy know what they were getting into when they shone the light of respect on Mary, the one woman that celibate clergy always revered as safe to love.

While I agree with Sara Robinson that patriarchal men are utterly petrified of birth control, I do not agree with her premise that "we will still be fighting about this 100 years from now." It is true that the change has only just begun, and that the patriarchy has been entrenched in our genetics for thousands of years. But the movement that has been made in consciousness over the past hundred years is exponential. It is rapid, rather than slowly linear.

DOWNTON ABBEY AND MONUMENTAL MOVEMENT

My husband and I became enthralled with the Downton Abbey Masterpiece Theater saga: The stories of those of the manor-born juxtaposed against the lives of their suffering servants. The era covers pre-World War I to Spanish flu and into the late 1920's. The patriarchal economic imprisonment of women was evident for both upstairs and downstairs. We saw the domination of women by men who controlled the purse strings. Women did not inherit the estate, while the distant male relative could. The patriarchy in power also kept the boundaries between servant and master. However, within a matter of ten years, World War I and the Spanish flu had blown apart staid manor. The boundaries between servant and master, women and men, were shifting. If we view Downton Abbey as our collective unconscious in microcosm, we see transformation arise from the ashes of grief of an old world lost, and from the trauma of war and death. But all in the span of less than a generation.

After many convolutions, we see Mary, the oldest daughter finally be reconciled with her true love, her cousin Matthew who will inherit the Manor. She has feared that because she had earlier compromised her honor by enjoying the amorous pursuit of the foreign guest who invites himself into her bedroom (and then dies!) that Matthew would not ever forgive her or even consider marrying her. Rather than being of the old patriarchal order, Matthew answers her entreaty with "will you ever forgive me?" With a "no—because there is nothing to forgive...we have lived our lives and now we are together." They stand there, shoulder to shoulder, looking out into a new and strange world, fraught with more trauma and crises ahead, the horrors of World War II yet to be experienced. Yet there is a movement to more consciousness, the boundaries of class weakening, the balance between the male and female growing. In Jungian terms, they are the *conjunctio oppositorum*—the joining of opposites, male and female. The *conjunctio* recognizes that wholeness arises from the joining of two equal yet opposite forces—the feminine and masculine.

At first glance, concepts of *conjunctio oppositorum*, the feminine principle, *anima*, and *animus*, the wounded feminine, may seem abstract and unknowable. Or that describing fiction through such terms is just one more trivial, intellectual exercise. But glance again into the world we live in, and we see we are bombarded on a daily basis by the theme of the rise of the wounded feminine principle against the dying patriarchy.

However, although the patriarchy's time is nigh, the

patriarchs still own the estate. The powers that be may still be The Titans. But Titans, as the myth reminds us, get inflated with their power and so were vanquished. I have always marveled at why large behemoth structures that were touted to be indomitable were named Titan...the Titanic, ... the Titan rocket. The myth of Titan is very apt as the story of pride before a fall. (The Titans lost power to the Olympians when they killed and dismembered Dionysus.)

3

THE ENVIRONMENT: WHO CARES?

We believe we can destroy our habitat without also destroying ourselves. How could we be so tragically wrong? (Kathleen Dean Moore, Sun Magazine, December, 2012.)

In 1962, Rachel Carson's book, *Silent Spring*, was published. This little book ushered in a shift of consciousness regarding the environment. It was here that Carson exposed the hazards of DDT, meticulously describing "how DDT entered the food chain and accumulated in the fatty tissues of animals, including human beings, and caused cancer and genetic damage." (Natural Resources Defense Council—NRDC—website.)

Truly a woman of heart whose voice needed to be heard, Carson loved and cared for not only nature but also her family. She was, as many women need be, a writer and researcher in the midst of caregiving. After her niece died, she adopted her five-year-old grand-nephew. Forging on with her work while she confronted breast cancer, she also cared for her ailing mother. This is often the woman's story, balancing worlds in our hearts, is it not? Bringing the care of hearth and home to embrace the human family ... .

The NRDC notes how aware Carson was of the "larger implications of her work." In fact, she was prepared for a backlash from the chemical industry and so her book contained a raft of documentation. In 1964, in a CBS documentary shortly before her death, Carson remarked, "Man's attitude toward nature is today critically important simply because we have now acquired a fateful power to alter and destroy nature. But man is a part of nature, and his war against nature is inevitably a war against himself. ... [We are] challenged as mankind has never been challenged before to prove our maturity and our mastery, not of nature, but of ourselves."

The challenge remains ... .

SALEM—AUG 12, 2012

Before I go to a Maine lake to write, we visit Salem, Massachusetts, looking for wedding venues for my daughter and her beau. The Peabody Essex Museum is our destination. We walk through the streets filled with witches' costumes, tarot readers, fortune tellers, kiosks of Goth jewelry, fantasy rings. How did Salem get here from that time in 1692 when fourteen women and six men were hung for being "witches?" Oh, I know, we are a capitalistic co-optive society in which past sins (not of the "witches" but of the people that hung them for trumped up crimes) are mollified if not nullified by making them into a money-maker. So we sell what we had condemned. On the other hand, in 1992, the Witch Trials memorial was dedicated by Nobel Laureate Elie Wiesel as part of the Tercentenary of the Witch Trials. Nevertheless, I think about this as I read Susan Griffin's prologue in *Women and Nature: The Roaring Inside Her*. How women have been for thousands of years cast as of the earth, and therefore, evil. Women are too natural, too herby, too earthy, too bloody: not enough sky god verticality. No rising phallus but a mysterious cave. Scary.

Mother—mater—matter—*materia*. I sit reading Susan Griffin's book *Women and Nature*, published in 1978. Yet, her words reverberate in this "new" millennium.

Worlds and words stack into each other like a Matrushka or nesting set of blocks—one fitting into another until all are stacked one inside the other. How can mother, matter, mater, *materia*, the Bhagavad Gita, and J. Robert Oppenheimer be so held in one container?

"I am become death, the shatterer of worlds" are the words spoken by Sri Krishna in the Bhagavad Gita. Susan Griffin notes that J. Robert Oppenheimer quotes this at the site of the first atomic blast. And it is my mother who told me that in the 1940's she believed she had a long conversation with Oppenheimer on a bus, headed to New York City. Getting on at Princeton, he sat down next to her. I was the toddler in her lap. (He may have even held me for a moment?) My mother would tell me this story often, always noting how sad this man appeared to be, how he seemed so regretful. Even as a child, my impression from her words was that Oppenheimer was the one man of the atom bomb project that had a sense of the moral (or immoral) immensity of the undertaking.

My mother herself thought the bombings of Hiroshima and Nagasaki to have been immoral. Later, in the early 1950's, my mother was also the one lonely voice in my extended family (or my town, for that matter) who lamented all the nuclear testing that was occurring in the Pacific atolls. She worried about the future of the earth and how we were upsetting the balance of nature. My mother was the irrelevant "kook" of her family who painted her tiny row house living room chartreuse and did kitschy oriental motif (ceramic Chinese ladies and men holding lampshades?!) while everyone else was faux (Leave It To Beaver) colonial.

Those who see what others cannot comprehend are often shooed away as irrelevant.

My mother was, in her irrelevance, a disenfranchised daughter of the patriarchy. She tried to play by its rules but never managed to. And for this I am profoundly grateful.

Because she, who did not finish high school, so that her brothers could go on to college, inculcated a love of earth and nature in my brother and me. Despite the fact we lived in a cramped space behind her store, it was evident my mother cared for the earth. She tended her little rose garden with care and later in life got to build a house on a wooded lot where she saved every pine tree she could. But most memorable was the time that a garter snake had wrapped itself around her ankle as she and I, a four-year-old, walked through some tall grass at my uncle's house. Uttering a simple, "Oh," she raised her leg and, with a swift kick, the snake flew off. In my child mind, she became a veritable earth-goddess. She later applauded my brother's conservation efforts to save the Pine Barrens of New Jersey.

As I recall my mother as snake-woman, I am sitting by a lake where loons call. Speed boats here are their nemesis. Again another microcosm of patriarchal power dominating the environment. There always needs to be a balance between the urge to dominate nature and nature's need to lead the way. More flow, less force. So the loons, who have been on the endangered list, cry out when there is a sense of any encroachment on their territory.

No, this is not about banning power boats, but about respecting the nature that everyone, including the birds, are here to enjoy. It always astounds me how humans are drawn to pictures of landscapes and are drawn to lakes and oceans and mountains and yet don't get the connection that in order to preserve these environments we all need to care for the planet as a whole. The stillness of the lake with its mirrored surface succumbs all too easily to the wake of the boat that passed by minutes before.

In 1998, Ed Ayres wrote in *World Watch* magazine:

The greatest destruction in our world is not being inflicted by psychopathic tyrants or terrorists. It's being done by ordinary people—law-abiding, church-going, family-loving, moral people—who are enjoying their sport-utility vehicles, their vaca-

tion cruises, and their burgers, and are oblivious to where those pleasures come from and what they really cost. Oblivious not to what those things cost at the store, but to what they cost when all the uncounted effects of their production and use are added up.

It's all connected. What happens upstream goes downstream. That plastic bottle thrown on the side of the road eventually gets washed to sea to become part of a dead zone of washed-up plastic that kills fish. We like to catch fish; we like to eat fish. Somehow the message has to become clear: the master-slave relationship of man subordinating nature will not work. We are literally killing ourselves in the attempt.

If we do not change our relationship to nature, the earth will not sustain us.

VIGNETTES OF DISCONNECT

One day, as I write, an acquaintance stops by my chair at the pond. Her son has a farm where he has initiated a CSA (Community Supported Agriculture). She tells me that she recently met a little grade school boy who said to her, "Why do we need farms? We just go to the grocery store."

I also recall my personal experience in a Western Pennsylvania steel town in 1974 when I worked at the community mental health program there. One day, driving to work, I see one of the many teenagers who came to our drop in center. As I stopped to pick him up and taken him into town, I remarked, "Wow, the pollution is really bad today." He looked at me with surprise, "What pollution?" The thick smoggy air was all this young man knew—so how could it be any different? Just like the grade schooler, the world he knew was disconnected from the larger picture. The teen was disconnected from fresh air; the boy was disconnected from earth's bounty. Their ignorance, innocent as it is, is nevertheless not bliss.

When we compartmentalize our thinking and don't consider the interconnectedness of all things, we easily lose sight of how what we do in one place has ramifications everywhere else.

The domination of nature is a direct outcome of patriarchy. And patriarchy's domination of nature goes hand in hand with its degradation and demeaning of both women and the feminine principle.

Susan Griffin wrote *Woman and Nature: The Roaring Inside Her* after she delivered a talk on women and ecology. She believes that often civilization's problems with nature is placed upon women to solve. She notes (p. xv):

Women were always asked to clean up. ... men consider women to be more material than themselves, or more a part of nature. The fact that man does not consider himself a part of nature, but indeed considers himself superior to matter, seemed to me to gain significance when placed against man's attitude that woman is both inferior to him and closer to nature.

Griffin elected to write her book in the feeling tone of

poetry rather than the so-called objective tone of patriarchal prose. Her complaint is that patriarchal thought claims to be objective and separate from emotion. She opted to dive beneath logic and enlist her intuition, her "uncivilized self" to ferret the feeling in the facts of history.

Her parody of the historical parade of patriarchy reminds us that what is of earth is decaying and corruptible. Poetically paraphrasing the patriarchal view, she says (p. 7-8):

And the demon resides in the earth, it is decided, in Hell, under our feet. It is observed that women are closer to the earth. That women lead to man's corruption. 'Woman are the Devil's Gateway,' it is said.

So, for thousands of years, women and earth are bound together to be the bane of men and patriarchy. Griffin reminds us that Eve was blamed for the Fall: it was she who was thought to take away earthly bliss, bringing upon earth mutability and decay. While Griffin considers patriarchy to be about the domination and demeaning of women and nature, I contend that patriarchy demeans and dominates not only nature, and women, but also denigrates the feminine principle that must be honored in all life. Patriarchy's suppression goes beyond gender.

However, my personal experience of motherhood (not to mention menses) attests to my sense of being connected to nature, earth and body.

I remember giving birth to my first child Zofia after a

forty-eight hour labor, which led to maternal and fetal distress, which led to Caesarean section. However, I was awake through it all so when the nurse brought my swaddled infant to me, I was able to nurse her. She and I somehow both intuited what to do and my breast for the first time fed her. This moment to me was as miraculous and memorable as was her birth. Later in the hospital room when she was brought to me, I laid her on my belly, close to the interior place where she had been for nine months. Now the formerly wombed wiggles of her legs and arms were seen as well as felt. I looked at her in awe.

Unfortunately, my son and I were separated from each other when he was born a preemie, so I didn't get to hold him right away. It took weeks before he was able to nurse.

Yet, for both babies, the experience of the body to body contact of nursing felt primal, grounding—yes, sometimes to the point of feeling like a cow in mud—but most times there was a sense of earthly wholeness. Not every woman experiences childbirth or nursing, but every woman experiences her connection to body and nature through the menstrual cycles. Women are in constant cycle with earth, blood, and body.

So, how much more perhaps a woman, whether conscious of it or not, is rooted to earth, matter, mater, *materia*. The feminine principle that needs to be integrated in both men and women arises from feminine connection to mater, matter, *materia*, earth.

Where the masculine energy is the vertical, the feminine energy is horizontal. In this depiction, the masculine rises

81

(like the phallus) skyward. In patriarchy, this vertical orientation is given priority and power (note sky scrapers!). The feminine, represented by the horizontal, earth plane, is considered lowly—of dirt, earth matter. Balance is attained by the interaction of the horizontal and vertical planes.

But this balance is negated in patriarchy. And so what is of the earth, of matter, is deemed inferior . Hence, both women and mother earth are subjugated and dominated.

The Clergy, the Clitoris, and Climate Change

So how is it that the clergy, the clitoris, and climate change are all related? First of all, I like the alliteration and it popped into my head at Quaker meeting one Sunday so I'm figuring the Holy Spirit got playful that morning.

Catholic clergy, represent just one subset of the patriarchal powers that demean both women and the feminine principle. However, they have been a vociferous lot who recently deflected their energies from their own sexual abuse cover-ups to blaming the nuns for focusing on the poor and on social justice rather than decrying, not only abortion, but also contraception. So they are not at all enamored with clitori because control of women's bodies for the sole purpose of procreation eliminates the need for pleasure (again, except for men).

The clitoris is that sexual pleasure part of a woman's anatomy that patriarchs aren't happy with. Patriarchs of the psyche didn't like it earlier—Freud and others were convinced that women should have vaginal and not clitoral orgasms. This view has been debunked all the way from

Masters and Johnson to Eve Ensler and beyond, yet there are cultures where girls and women are brutally maimed by so-called circumcision of the clitoris.

Nicholas Kristof's and Sally Woo Dunn's interviews with girls and women so affected were referred to in a previous chapter. Of note also is the novel, *Cutting for Stone*, by Ethiopian born medical doctor and author Abraham Verghese. His fictional work confronts the reality of female "circumcision" and all its painful side effects.

In addition to female genital manipulation (FGM), Verghese's characters also suffer the results of fistulas. While FGM is not the major contributor to the occurrence of fistulas (holes), poverty and lack of adequate obstetric care are. The Fistula Foundation describes an obstetric fistula as a hole between a woman's birth passage and one or more of her internal organs, such as the bladder or rectum. They are caused by prolonged labor; and can also be the result of rape. The result of a fistula is permanent incontinence of urine or feces or both. Women in developing countries suffer not only the medical problems, but also suffer by being ostracized by their communities.

If women's bodies are solely vessels for the purpose of procreation, and pleasure is only for men, then the clitoris is only a vestigial organ not unlike an inflamed appendix.

If the patriarchy demeans and violates women, seeing them as needing to be dominated and subjugated, then it is not so great a leap to see that the patriarchy also dominates and subjugates Mother Earth. If the feminine principle were in balance, the earth would not be pillaged and raped. But our feminine ground may wreak vengeance upon us for the climate change we have wrought.

Climate change is the result of our plundering. We dig deep into the earth and under the sea for oil and gas and coal and minerals. We spew toxins into the air. We clear cut timberland. We manufacture megatons of stuff, then throw away tons more.

We can't do violence with Mother Earth and think she will take our abuse forever. The queendom of Kali shall come if we continue our abusive relationship with nature. The Indian Hindu goddess Kali is that aspect of the Divine that is feminine, but Kali is both nurturing and destructive. She brings life and death, water and floods, calm earth and quaking earth, solid mountains and volcanic eruptions. However, the life-death-life cycle has been set off course by us.

I remember meeting Joanna Macy at a conference almost fifteen years ago. She is the "deep ecologist," who, like Rachel Carson before her, sings the warning like the proverbial canary in the coal mine: our global environment is in deep trouble.

When I first heard Joanna Macy speak, I was convinced that surely governments, people, even corporations would come together in unity to change the course of climate change. I thought, surely, with the evidence mounting, that industrialization has caused devastating changes in our world, that we as humans could reverse the exponential movement of our warming globe. How naïve I was to be optimistic about our collective response to the truths she told. She knew then that few were listening, yet she contin-ues delivering her message even today.

I catch myself at how I don't listen and observe; and I see how other people don't listen either. It's summer. I'm at the Pond for my daily swim and I notice as I look up from the water that the life guard is spraying the sandy beach. I yell up to him, "Hey, are you killing off the mining bees?" He says, "Well, yes, there are some nests in the sand over here." I implore him to stop since these bees don't sting and are helpful, eating up other insects. Also, the bee population is in danger and are suffering decimation with bee colonies collapsing: the result of that is no pollination of flowers and crops.

Go to any state agricultural extension website or any horticultural program and you will find the same story about mining bees. The University of Rhode Island Land-scape Horticultural Program notes that, while the presence of numerous mining bees flying close to the ground may be a "nuisance for some people," they are not aggressive and rarely, if ever, sting. Mining bees are "solitary" not hav-ing long-lived colonies or a large nest with one queen bee. Instead, each female digs her own burrow to rear her young. Every web site where I read about mining bees, concurred with the University of Rhode Island that mining bees are extremely beneficial insects, important for pollination. Their burrowing may also be beneficial by aerating the soil. Given that the activity is extremely brief, and that the males cannot sting at all, and that the honey bee populations have been suffering colony collapse, I find it a travesty that my oasis of nature, the pond, can act so aggressively against the natural world.

There is an interconnectedness that is denied every time we act on our own myopic vision.

Later, I tell the Pond manager about the mining bees and what they do. He is unaware of their utility. I then remind him of how I no longer see bats swooping over the water at night to catch mosquitos—and that is probably because there is a fungus that is wiping out entire populations of bats. (I talk about this in more detail later on in this chapter.) So all the more do we need the mining bees to do their job dragging the gnats and mosquitos into the bees' sandy hideaways. Again not to mention we need the bees to pollinate so we can eat.

We seem so clueless about what we are doing—or not doing—in our world. We are, especially in the U.S., a throwaway society. My pond is my microcosm of study. Not only do people know nothing of the good of mining bees or the plight of bats, they also seem blind to the sign on the can that says, "Recycle!" Invariably, lots of recyclables get pitched with the rest of the trash. Not that we're so virtuous when we feel the need to use plastic in the first place. All those plastic bottles are problematic to the environment, recycled or no.

And I don't mean to castigate others from any plastic-free tree perch. I include myself as ecology's sinner. I am waking to Joanna Macy's words more and more.

ROSE GARDENS AND FRACKING

How ironic that Pennsylvania Governor Corbett's wife Susan is featured on the front page of the Philadelphia Inquirer in her rose garden (not to be mistaken for the teeny one my mother had) while the governor is wooing oil and gas companies with sweet tax breaks so that they will (and have) come to "frack" the you know what out of the Marcellus Shale beds. There should be a huge outcry about what this fracking will do (and has done already in some areas) to the water supply, and to the environment in general. Fracking uses chemicals and water to extract natural gas from shale. Rather than consider the destruction of underground water sources and denuding the land, Corbett is riding his own political bulldozer, running roughshod over any dissent. He also doesn't seem to care a whit about the infrastructure that is being degraded by heavy truck traffic. This is clearly a negative masculine thrust with no thought or feeling but the bottom line. Hence it is unbridled power without relationship to the feminine principle and connection to both community ("Commonwealth") and conservation.

Hmm, words! Ever notice how conservatives are the opposite of conservationists and that in my state, which is a "commonwealth," no thought is given to the common good?

Meanwhile Susan Corbett smiles for the camera in her rose garden. Yet another daughter of the patriarchy letting us know that she cares lovingly for gardens and all things beautiful while her husband plunders the earth where she doesn't live. A little corner of nature protected from his bulldozer. Despite the blooms in the garden, neither Corbett is brimming with feminine principle.

Emma Jung held that when the animus and anima (and the anima in particular) are acknowledged appropriately, that the feminine principle blossoms. This, she notes, is not only important for the individual, but for being in right relationship with the natural world (p. 87):

When the anima is recognized and integrated a change of attitude occurs toward the feminine generally. This new evolution of the feminine principle brings with it a due reverence for nature, too; whereas the intellectual viewpoint dominant in an era of science and technology leads to utilizing and even exploiting nature, rather than honoring her. Fortunately, signs can be observed today pointing in the latter direction. Most important and significant of these is probably the new dogma of the Assumptio Mariae and her proclamation as mistress of creation. In our time, where such threatening forces of cleavage are at work, splitting peoples, individuals and atoms, it is doubly necessary that those which unite and hold together should become effective; for life is founded on the harmonious interplay of masculine and feminine forces, within the individual human being as well as without. Bringing these opposites into union is one of the most important tasks of present-day psychotherapy.

Emma Jung wrote this in 1955. We have had much change

since then that affirms her words; on the other hand, we have also had much change back—climate change, for one, is the result of our continuing the dominator stance over nature.

Joanna Macy continues to remind us that we are interdependent or, as Buddhist monk Thich Nhat Hanh would say, we are inter-being.

The sense of separate self is what creates illusory distance from our suffering world and wounded environment. Macy is first to admit that separation of self from nature, the individual from the collective, has brought much good. She allows that "The distanced and observing eye brought us tools of science, and a priceless view of the vast, orderly intricacy of our world. The recognition of our individuality brought us trial by jury and the Bill of Rights." (Joanna Macy, *World As Lover, World As Self*, p 13)

Yet if we continue to lurch toward evermore independence and separateness, we lose our grounding and are out of balance. To rectify the imbalance, Macy summons us to re-connect with our interdependence. This is, in essence, attending to the rise of the wounded feminine, to the feminine principle of relationship that has been forgotten for so long.

Macy's theme is about deep ecology, in other words, not about band-aid fixes to environmental issues but a whole new (or perhaps re-found) perspective of relationship to the environment. In the mid-1970's, Macy tells us that Norwegian philosopher and mountain climber Arne Naess coined the term, "deep ecology," to contrast it with discrete, "short-term fixes" (p. 13):

> ... short term, technological fixes, band-aid approaches to ecological problems, ... do not address the sources of these problems, which is our stance in relation to our world. What is destroying our world is the persistent notion that we are independent of it, aloof from other species, and immune to what we do to them. Our survival, Naess says, requires shifting into more encompassing ideas of who we are.

In other words, we must come home to honoring the feminine principle, healing the wounded feminine within us all, the eros of the universe to rise again. This means finding that which is in ourselves to meet the world in ways we have dismissed and forgotten. For the feminine principled, we meet the world not as other, but as self. Seeing the world as lover, world as self is the invitation (Macy, p. 11):

> ... when you see the world as lover, every being, every phenomenon, can become ... an expression of that ongoing, erotic impulse. It takes form right now in each one of us and in everyone and everything we encounter—the bus driver, the clerk at the checkout counter, the leaping squirrel.

As I write this, I am visited first by a loon plunging long and deep to find its nourishment in the lake. Then a hummingbird comes to call. Wings beating loudly, it hovers at my face. Okay, birds of nature, I will let the human "interbeings" know that you are here hoping they will heed the call for honoring the feminine principle.

If they do, your world, our world, we, are on our way to healing the great woundedness of the earth.

Ah the loon has lifted her head from the watery depths. I am comforted to know that she is still here.

LOON ON LONG LAKE

Sunrise calm
Loon arrives discreetly.
Fishing, she dives down
Taking her time in the deep.
What fullness of breath she has
To be able to plunge the dark
To find her nourishment.
Would that I could do likewise.

PLUNGING INTO THE DARK OF WINTER, JOURNAL ENTRY, JANUARY, 2012

At home, I hear my neighbor sneeze. The windows are closed, yet I hear him. "God bless you," I say silently. Just minutes earlier another neighbor (at least I hope it was a neighbor) fired a shot at some animal he was hunting. I assume he was in the marshy woods across the street, yet it felt so close; and. at that same moment, something fell past my window by the computer where I was sitting. It was not the bird he shot, but a leaf. Perhaps the vibration and shock of the sound shook not only me but also the leaf.

And why not? Everything, at its deepest level, is connected. Our disconnect is the denial. High school was a shattering of worlds for me. It started with the sudden death of my cousin at the age of thirteen—I was fourteen. I vividly recall the phone call from the hospital that Thanksgiving night. We already knew that Roger was hit while he was riding his bike, delivering newspapers in an icy rain. Brain damaged, he lingered into the night. My childhood belief in miracles and the remoteness of death carried me until the call of finality. I remember sobbing into the pillow, devastated at my human helplessness, defeated by mortality. How could anyone so young die first? Death, death, no bounds, no rules.

Assumptive worlds blown asunder. Life is so fragile, mortality ever at our shoulder, even as children. My parents, having grown up in a world without penicillin and surviving the flu of 1918 knew this already, of course. And my mother had suffered several miscarriages before she gave birth to me (hence the almost eleven-year difference in age between my brother and me). My father knew death early too. His mother had miscarriages and there was also a child who died a crib death. My paternal grandmother herself died at a fairly young age when my father was in his twenties. Generations before me know the fragility of life well, as do people in the developing world and in the inner city right now. I did not until I was fourteen. So that was one huge paradigm shift for me.

Another paradigm shift—a turning upside down of my assumptive world—was chemistry class. Suddenly, the mystical and poetic wedded to the wonders of science. I wasn't all that enamored with the nitty gritty of chemistry. (later, I became a chemistry major, more for the poetic romance of it, after all Kekule dreamt benzene rings). I was in love with seeing the world as a vibrancy of atoms touching one another everywhere with nothing being separate, with beholding the universe as one. Oh what a delight that was to consider that everything was/is connected in a floating sea of movement of electrons. Energy everywhere. All one. I liked that distinctions of table vs chair were arbitrary. That my cup, if only I had the electron-microscope eyes for it, was a mass of atomic energy, one with the hand that held it. Flow more than form. Yumm. This paradigm shift was much more embraceable than facing my mortality.

Okay, so where is this meandering memoir going? Perhaps facing mortality, not denying death and seeing how all is connected, is connected. Of course, we need to view the world more mechanically, our everyday lives are more Newtonian physics, less quantum mechanics, so that the table, the chair, the cup can have clear and distinct boundaries. We can manage mundane existence. Yet we can get so constricted by the compartmentalization that we forget the interconnections.

My spouse adds his own witness of worlds:

Kayta, we live at several levels of abstraction. When typing this, I'm barely aware that there is program (Word) receiving my input and formatting it, that Word uses the operating system to store this info to disk, that the operating system deals with memory, both disk and "RAM," how this translates to 1's and 0's, stored and retrieved, using different physical phenomena in these cases but ultimately related to stuff at a more and more "fundamental" level. But are the details fundamental, or are the thoughts expressed (and evoked while reading it) the more fundamental?

Noticing interconnections, certainly to the relationships among things is more of the "feminine" principle than the masculine sense of logical categories and compartmentalization. Granted both are needed to live. However, we need to maintain a balance of focus. Looking at life through the lens of logical delineations between chair and table is necessary but not sufficient. (There's logic for you right there—logic bites its own tail.) We also need the lens that sees beyond the distinctions to the connection of all things.

AND DECEMBER, 2012?

Tonight I approach the TV with remote control in hand, to watch the Cassandra of Cable, Amy Goodman and *Democracy Now*. Amy is the only female TV anchor I've ever seen who avoids lipstick and voices the hard truths that others avoid. I see her today standing in the cold of Oslo, Norway, after the Nobel Peace Prize had been awarded to the European Union. Well, why not give a peace prize to a whole pride of patriarchs. After all, the United States Supreme Court has deemed corporations to be persons. Bewildering as all that is, it is not as mind boggling as the stories Amy Goodman covered recently when she was in Doha for the climate change summit. While her cohorts in the states were perseverating their eyeballs off over the "Fiscal Cliff," Amy Goodman was busy interviewing the global community about their concerns regarding climate change. This is our most critical issue and yet the American powers that be continue to give it short shrift, even after Superstorm Sandy has devastated New York and New Jersey.

America diluted the final United Nation resolutions, making for a weak solution. No strong medicine here. Developing nations who are already reeling from the impact of climate change—severe weather, rising sea levels, etc., are once again beholden to the brawny bullies on the block.

With the Doha Climate Gateway "deal," the United States made no new pledge to cut its emissions or to increase aid to nations suffering from the impact of climate change, noted Amy Goodman. Not only did the Doha Meeting come on the heels of Superstorm Sandy, it coincided with Typhoon Bopha, wreaking havoc in the Phillipines, with hundreds of people dead and thousands more missing. In Doha, after the end of the talks, Goodman interviewed Kumi Naidoo of Greenpeace International. He passionately stated:

> Our governments must realize that this failure is a betrayal of the people in the Philippines and around the world that have faced climate impacts now, today, and will continue in the days to come. But what is at stake here is not some ethereal thing called the planet, the climate, the environment, but what is at stake here is selling down our children and grandchildren's futures.

Later, in Oslo, Goodman interviewed Samantha Smith, the leader of the World Wildlife Fund's Global Climate and Energy Initiative. (Note that in the US this is simply known as the World Wildlife Fund.) She, too, strongly voiced her concern saying:

This was an incredibly weak deal. ... there is just not yet enough of a sense of moral outrage about the impacts of climate change. ... Climate change affects the poorest people in the poorest country. ... This is not just a problem for a few people. ... [and the United States played] an incredibly disappointing role.

Riding Uncle Sam's coattails, Canada helped blockade financial aid for developing countries and pulled out of the Kyoto Protocol. Loons may be symbolized on the Canadian dollar as representing a love of nature; but nature is, apparently, not this nation's bottom line either. Listen! The loons cry out for all of us. Stories of warming abound.

FROM BATS TO FARMS

Recently on NPR, Steve Curwood, in his *Living On Earth* program, interviewed (January 25, 2013) Katie Gillies, the Imperiled Species Coordinator of Bat Conservation International. She noted that entire bat populations are becoming extinct due to a fungal disease, white nose syndrome, which affects the respiratory system. Fox News doesn't care and who listens to *Living On Earth* at 6 AM, I wonder? The facts are available but not disseminated to the masses. Bats earn their weight, not in gold, but in ingesting thousands of insect pests each night. It is estimated that the bats' insect eating provides a twenty-three billion dollar benefit to farmers each year. They are the farmers' friends—protecting crops from pests in quite an economical way—not to mention eating the mosquitoes that bite our legs in the evening twilight. Perhaps when the economic ramification of their demise becomes clear, people will care. Again I am reminded of how no one cared about the grape pickers' illnesses due to pesticide contact until Cesar Chavez, leader of the Farm Workers Movement, warned the consumers that the pesticides were not good for their health either. Until we see we are all related we only care about our closest relations. And some of us only relate to ourselves.

From Farm to Table

Even half listening to Lynn Rosetta Kasper's *The Splendid Table* on NPR (January 25, 2013) had me cursing Monsanto once again. Recently she talked about seed saving in India. Traditionally, farmers saved their seeds from year to year, but then came industrial agriculture a la Monsanto, for example, which commandeered the farmer to produce crops for which he needed to buy new seeds every year. Kasper interviewed "Perennial Plate" duo, chef Daniel Klein and producer Mirra Fine, who are visiting farms and home kitchens and fishing boats across the globe.

Before their trip to India, they did some research and discovered that there have been over 200,000 farmers in the last 15 years who have suicided. One precipitating factor to this tragedy is that farmers are going into debt and losing their land. Underlying the debts is the fact that Indian farmers had to buy seeds every year. This occurred when corporations arrived selling seeds and removing traditional seeds from the market. These company-protected seeds cannot be used again.

There is now a movement initiated by Dr. Vandana Shiva to return to seed saving. Both Shiva and her colleague Bija Vidyapeeth are working to defeat Monsanto in India by introducing traditional varieties of rice. (Ironically, or perhaps synchronistically, *bija* means *seed* in Hindi.)

Thousands of years history resides in these seeds, remarks Daniel Klein. There is hereditary resilience when farmers save the strong seeds year-to-year. Such resilience was evident when the Eastern side of India was hit by the tsunami and farmers could not grow their usual crops due to the salt on the land. Saved, salt-resistant rice varieties were reintroduced to these farmers and the crops flourished.

Shiva and Vidyapeeth are women of heart in India who are being heard, saving seeds to save the planet.

4

ON MONEY AND THE FEMININE PRINCIPLE

*I don't mind you being rich. I mind you **Buying** my government. (Occupy Wall St Protestor's Sign (Barlett and Steele, p. 30))*

It is difficult to extricate myself from patriarchal permeations/pervasiveness. I am, even if swimming against the tide, still swimming in the patriarchy's pool. We all live in patriarchy like a school of fish swims in waters or a flock of birds flies. Patriarchal power is the air we breathe and it is polluted with the grime and crime of greed and rigidity and judgment. So we, just as the gentle male dreamer, in a previous chapter, feel guilt and fear if we try to filter the water or the air that is our atmosphere. This is as literal as it is metaphoric.

It is amazing how patriarchy so resists the science of climate change and doesn't care a whit about polluting the air and water as long as money keeps flowing. Yet another myth of Midas. Recall that for Midas everything turned to gold. That is an unlivable situation—money so disconnected from life is deadening: the golden apple cannot nourish, the golden wife cannot love.

Not wanting to be without life, I turn to Helen Luke whenever I wonder how my thought might delve psychologically deeper. She, fortunately (fortune, aha), has written an essay about money that I think is relevant to our times.

She reminds us that the word "money" is derived from the Latin *moneta*, which means mint or money and whose origins come from the name of the goddess and her temple where Roman coins were minted (p. 43):

> *It is significant indeed that the goddess from whose temple, from whose womb, so to speak, sprang the coinage of our civilization has sunk into obscurity and is forgotten, while the money which was dedicated to her has acquired an ever increasing autonomous power and is worshipped unashamedly as an end in itself.*

Note that money was minted in the temple of a goddess not a god: "For money is a symbolic means of exchange and therefore belongs to the feminine principle of relatedness."

Luke warns us that when the goddess factor (and I don't mean Ayn Rand) of relatedness in money is missing, we are in dire danger. There is in the relatedness, a transpersonal component that renders meaning to every exchange between people and in every realm, be it physical, emotional, spiritual or financial.

In terms of money, if we dismiss the transpersonal energy of the exchange, call it the divine if you can, then money is dissociated from relationship. Money becomes the love object. "...the love of divinity at the heart of the exchange turns into the love of money itself, which, in the words of Timothy in one of his epistles, is 'the root of all evil.'"

It is not money itself that is evil—but our attitude towards it that is the problem. When we sunder money from its "meaning as an exchange between people in valuing *feeling* values, then we begin to love money for its own sake or for the sake of that which we can gain from it, either possession is or security or, worst of all, power." (p. 44) These are hair-raising words asking us to raise our consciousness—and our consciences too.

Think of the words we use regarding money—contracts; stocks; shares; exchanges. Our notion of money has been literally <u>uprooted</u> from its mother earth meaning. Helen Luke notes that what used to be a com–pact has been overridden by a con–tract. Where a compact is "an agreement based on feeling values, a coming together in peace, *cum pace*," a contract is devoid of human feeling. It is a binding financial or legal agreement, nothing else. And "when compact becomes contract within us, man begins to earn without paying, or pay without earning, and money is divorced from the meaning of exchange."

Look at how abstracted wealth has become from work.

Worth in this landscape has little to do with work. Quite the opposite. Some of the hardest working people earn the least. Meanwhile, money works for itself: money makes money, gold breeds gold, but to what end? We are stocked with stocks and in bondage to bonds.

"Stock," while it has multiple meanings, has its root(!) in referring to "the main trunk of a tree or plant onto which grafts are made." But stock can also refer to an individual's "roots"—to be one of sound stock—what we inherit from our ancestors. However, "when autonomous money becomes the stock upon which the life of a man or a society is grafted, the rot begins." To paraphrase Luke, our market place is no longer, connected to earth and hands, full of the life of a bountiful harvest but has become "money markets" and "stock exchanges"—the trading of the "commodities" or grain is no closer to that which is grown in the earth than Jupiter is to Mars.

Helen Luke says it more cogently: "Something is to be had for nothing by the clever playing of the markets, and this is the absolute negation of exchange" (*ibid*, p 46).

"Share" no longer means to share with another as we tell our toddlers to do, but with how many shares of the "pie" we can have so that others have none. Share is now an acquisition.

Trust me (though I have no trusts) that I don't believe (nor does Helen Luke) that the answer is to swing on the pendulum to revolutionary zeal. We cannot live communally without reckoning with our own internal greed. And I fully admit to my own psychological complexes and family mythology about money and deprivation/depression mentality. And so I, as do we all, need to do the work of examining my/our consciousness and conscience about my/our attitude toward money. With every individual who does his or her own interior work of growth of consciousness, the outer world is that much closer to a more enlightened awareness.

Wise elder woman Luke reminds us that while we need to see clearly the true evil of a "money-dominated" society, we also need to maintain the responsibility for what money symbolizes: the give and take of paying and earning. "Exchange is never exclusive," she remarks. Such a pithy remark for a profound insight. What she means by this is exchange is a reciprocal responsibility that goes beyond our own group, our own tribe or commune or community or nation. It is also a reciprocal responsibility so that no one feels he owes nothing to society: e.g., the CEO would no longer have the distorted notion that he made it on his own. It also means that no one can feel society owes him everything either because of a sense that money is evil. Luke alerts us to the need for honest human exchange so that we are not corrupted by money—no matter our socio-economic status.

I recall a financial planner extolling the virtues of Sam Walton (Walmart founder) because he arranged for his family, with all their wealth, to pay absolutely no inheritance tax. This planner thought what a great deed that was. I thought, no, what great greed that was!

Many of us complain about "taxes" and Helen Luke by

no means suggests that we not allow ourselves legitimate ways to reduce our tax load. But she does define our relationship with taxes psychologically, showing us that our resentments about paying taxes may arise from our own "unfaced shadow qualities" which then become our own evasions of the responsibilities of true exchange (p. 52):

People who would cry out in horror when a man cheats his neighbor or refuses to pay his debts may grin when telling you how they have just hatched up a new plot to evade taxation. ... If we really think deeply, taxation emerges as one of the greatest ideas that humankind has ever conceived. It is the means whereby people live in community with each other while still retaining freedom of choice in most of their spending and earning. Without taxation there must be dictatorship or anarchy. As on all levels of exchange, the sacrifice of a degree of freedom ensures the essential freedom.

When I heard Ira Glass's "This American Life" (March 2, 2012, transcript 459 on NPR), Helen Luke's words about taxes and communal responsibility resounded. The theme of the radio program was "What kind of America do we want?" Underneath the perennial political fight over taxes is the polarity between desire for a "smaller, cheaper U.S. vs. a bigger, 'taxier' U.S."

Glass notes how, in 2009, Springfield, Illinois, state police had to do away with their motorcycle division due to budget cuts. The result? Far more motorcycle fatalities.

Moving on to Trenton, one of the show's producers,

Sarah Koenig interviews Sergeant Mark Kieffer. Due to budget cuts by New Jersey Governor Chris Christie, Trenton laid off 103 police officers. That was one-third of their force. Result? Sgt. Kieffer noted 15-20 robberies a week where there had previously been five. Detectives in the robbery unit went from eight to two and in thirty-eight days, there were thirty-two shootings. Yes, Trenton had known crime before the cuts, but the marked increase was unprecedented. Koenig talked to residents that had only read about criminal activity in the news, now the experience was direct, no matter the neighborhood.

Trentonian Michael Walker has been an informal spokesperson of concern, going to meetings, starting a blog. He notes, "I think smaller government is a myth." Although his income last year was only $34,000, he is willing to pay more taxes to make Trenton a safer, cleaner city. However, others are concerned that the taxes collected are already mismanaged. Some attest that if they could be certain tax money was used wisely they might consider paying more.

Juxtapose taxes against a cable bill. Koenig notes that cable costs $159/month. That much in taxes would pay for 600 more Trenton police.

Perhaps some people are more willing to have cable than safety and infrastructure after all. Batten down the hatches, and watch "reality" TV—or a crime show or two.

Leaving the locked doors of Trenton, Ira Glass reports that every Republican running for national and statewide office takes a pledge, invented by Grover Norquist, to never increase taxes. This is part of Norquist's ultimate design to reduce the size of government (in his more "colorful" words, "I just want to shrink it down to the size where we can drown it in the bathtub.")

Yet, Ira Glass states (using percentages that apply to the marginal rate of taxation, not the overall taxation rate):

> *Our nation's current mania for cutting the size of government, keeping taxes low, is coming at a moment when our tax rates are, in fact, at one of the lowest levels in the last seventy years. The top personal income bracket paid over 80% of its income in the 1950's and 1960's, 70% when Ronald Reagan took office, 39% at the end of the Clinton years. Now it is 35%, ... Our taxes make up a smaller portion of the gross domestic product than taxes in most industrialized countries. ... it can seem very strange that this is a time when politicians are so unwilling to raise taxes, with all kinds of unintended consequences everywhere.*

Grover Norquist can, and does, boast that "his side" is winning.

Also part of the program, Robert Smith (of Planet Money, another NPR show) goes to Colorado Springs, Colorado. Home of Focus on the Family, this is a conservative's conservative city. Because the residents voted "no" to any tax increases, many services, including street lights, were shut down.

Smith observes that eventually some services got outsourced and privatized. Even though it would be more cost effective to have the municipality handling the services, with more services operative (e.g., the community swimming pools), people were pleased that "the government is doing less." The citizens are getting less and paying more but that illogic is trumped by the illusion of Norquist's dream.

City Councilwoman Jan Martin tells Smith the following story:

> ... *a gentleman came up to me and actually thanked me for the adopt a street light program. He had just written a check to the city for $300 to turn all the street lights back on in his neighborhood. And I did remind him that for $200, if he had supported the tax initiative, we could have had not only street lights, but parks and firemen and swimming pools and community centers. That by combining our resources, we as a community can actually accomplish more than we as individuals.*

Sigh, the man said he would still not support a tax increase. Jan Martin believes that is because of a lack of trust in "government." And I say that we have been brainwashed to believe that rugged individualism is our ingrained myth.

Two years later, after these interviews, Robert Smith returns to find Colorado Springs looking somewhat better; tax revenue was going up, but the experiment of less government continues. Nevertheless, this Colorado tourist town could be the prototype in our country screaming for "small government." The point of this story is that outsourcing what keeps our civilization going—street lights lit, garbage collected, roads fixed, and schools open—saves nothing and in the end costs more.

Councilwoman Martin is a staunch Republican, yet she saw this unraveling happening in her community. There is the key word: "community." Of course, we don't want our public servants spending money frivolously on upscale dinners or flights of fancy, and, of course, we want efficiency. However, we also need to recognize that civilization is not really about rugged individualism but about interconnectedness. We really do need each other to survive. Human beings have gotten as far as they have because they in fact do help each other and know they are interconnected. True, tribal and national loyalties against other tribes and nations may create animosities among us but as the globe becomes more and more connected, we must realize that rugged individualism is even less an option than it was two hundred years ago.

The one versus the many has been a perennial problem probably prior to Plato. Philosophers have studied this, family therapists see it at work. We belong to groups, we belong to families. We rely on this belonging for identity as well as survival. Yet, on the other hand, we all need to differentiate ourselves as individuals outside our context of family as well as other groups. Individuals must take responsibility for their actions and find an inner compass of conscience and authority. As a clinician, I have seen clients who must differentiate from their families of origin in order to discover their autonomy and to develop their own personhood. Being in community and collaboration does not run counter to being one's own authority. This is where the balance lies—honoring the tension between the "I" and the "we." Perhaps, instead of looking to patriarchal business models for how to run government into the ground, why not look at success in relationships? In order to work, relationships rely on the balance between the "I" and the "we." Both individuals must have their own autonomy—the I's—as well as connection—"we." The relationship is rich and strong when both poles are honored. There is interactive complementarity.

Such complementarity is also necessary in governing where we can respect the individual's freedom and autonomy while also recognizing responsibility to the "we" which is community.

AYN RAND AND THE I

Ayn Rand confronted her traumatic history of the Russian revolution by being dramatically opposed to all that rang "collective." She was born Alisa Rosenbaum in 1905 to a wealthy, prominent, and well-placed Jewish family. When the Bolsheviks came into power, the silver spoon with which she was born was wrenched away. Her father lost his pharmaceutical practice and their life was torn asunder. Despite Ayn Rand's eschewing of anything smacking of altruism, she herself was not without help along the way. Relatives in Chicago offered refuge to the family and her parents decided it was best for their Alisa, who had been sulky and taciturn, to take advantage of the offer. Always believing that she would some day become famous, Alisa was on her way out of Russia and into a new life. The seeds of her belief in the "I" against the "we," had already been planted. Her disdain of altruism and her love of logic and will, *a la* the Nietzsche she so admired, was set.

In her over-weighted demands for the "I," Rand has given us more fodder for our collective (hmmm!) narcissism. How about that? Some of the "we" (a goodly Grover Norquistian per cent) has come together in "community" to decry the need for community. The rugged individualists are banding together to keep solipsism alive, giving new meaning to "all for one, one for all."

Rand, the capitalist ideologue writer, may be the founding mother of the libertarian movement we see today. She certainly is the woman behind such capitalist men as Alan Greenspan, Paul Ryan, and Rush Limbaugh. However, she may be turning over in her grave about how some of her acolytes have chosen her capitalist ideology of the market yet thrown out her views on the equality of women, her atheism, and the place of civil liberty!

She championed the individual above all else and her faith was in a capitalism grounded in "reason" and "objectivity." She gave short shrift to emotions—the "irrational"—and pooh-poohed instincts which were to be vanquished by free will.

In Jungian terms, I think she was the negative animus woman *par excellence*, because she sought to be so one-dimensional. Yet I do not mean to demonize her or to dismiss her importance.

But while I think Rand was quite a heroine in her own

life, undaunted by whatever obstacles she encountered, I also think she was blinded by her own grandiosity and blunted by the virtue of her reliance on "reason." Our virtue is our vice, after all, and her "virtue of selfishness," left to its own devices is indeed a vice.

Jungian analyst James Hollis reminds us that Jung's notion of individuation from the collective is not at all about selfishness and self interest (p. 86, *On This Journey We Call Our Life*). In fact, while individuation means differentiating from the collective psyche of family and culture, it does not mean cut off and isolation. Unfortunately, Rand rationalized the need to be the "rugged individual" needing help from no one. Not one of us has ever gotten anywhere without the help of someone, even if it is as simple and anonymous as the bus driver who drops us off to work. Every step of our lives involves the interaction with others. Ironically, Rand had plenty of help from her family to set her on her way.

She did not seem to grow in consciousness to see that life is beyond reason and will. That our woundedness does need to be met with connection and compassion.

Actually, her personal life was the contradiction to her claims to reason. She may have projected onto her long-suffering husband, Frank O'Connor, her own need within of a gentle masculine presence that was kind and connected. She, under her assertiveness and independence-or-be-damned persona, needed an empathic relationship to bolster her.

Jennifer Burns notes in her biography of Ayn Rand, *Goddess of the Market* (p. 196):

When she traveled to distant places, she preferred to have the collective with her, or at least Frank.... ... Few understand how vital Frank's presence was to Rand. If it would benefit objectivism, she would go through the rituals and forms of being famous and expose herself to the public eye. But she needed Frank there with her, a comforting shield against the world.

While Rand may have been as needy for emotional attachment and connection as the rest of us, her persona is what lives on in capitalism's collective unconscious. Even the little guy may carry her ideology unknowingly within.

MEANDERINGS ABOUT THE LITTLE GUY: THE EVERYMAN AT THE BREWERY

The other night in the parking lot of a micro-brewery, I spied a small, oldish, quite seasoned car on whose rusted bumper was a sticker supporting Mitt Romney. Perhaps this person came from Massachusetts, say, and was happy with "Romney Care." More than likely that is not the case. This person, unless he is simply eschewing his trust fund, is not in the top one percent. Given the looks of the car and its contents, I would bet he is lucky not to be in the bottom of the bottom half (the 47% perhaps). And yet, he (yes, I think this car did belong to a guy), declares his allegiance to a very conservative ideology that has no mind to be concerned for his welfare.

Why? Why do people in little row houses or who may even be on unemployment or welfare or medicare vote against themselves time and time again?

It is a fact that many people actually believe they are going to be closer to the top than they actually will be. Or as the *New Yorker* cartoon of one-percenters say to each other—the "wannabees" are under the illusion that they have a chance in hell to "be."

So those that admit they are clearly at the bottom rung, still believe that if they win the lottery tomorrow all will be well and that they will "move on up." To protect themselves in that happy event, they align their vote with the few folks that are already there. Besides isn't it more fun to identify yourself with the celebrities and moguls at the top than with the "peon" next door? And if there is anyone on the rung below, well they're the ones to kick off, right? Because they may win that lottery ticket first, and that just won't do.

So kick off the poorer, or the immigrant, or the undocumented worker. Meanwhile that trickle down you feel from the top? Guess what that might be.

Of course, the media that is controlled by big money (Rupert Murdoch, Koch brothers, and so on) such as Fox News, instills fear in the little guy in order to keep the illusion going. So the yellow journalists report, in dire terms and with breathless voice, how big government is stealing their freedom, how we must have liberty and free enterprise to make America working again. The "enemy" of the people is the "other"—those who look foreign to basically white people, especially white males. And the "enemy" in collusion with this "other" is "my government."

The spuriousness of this ersatz ideology is so blatant it's painful to even feel the need to address it. There is no rocket science, no high math in understanding how nonsensical these claims of the right wing media are. Brain surgery might help, however, because it does seem that media pundits (painful to give them this much credit), such as Rush Limbaugh, do not want to reach their audience's pre-frontal cortex where executive functioning lies. What these TV and radio celebrities are after is the limbic system—the amygdala, in particular. It is fear they wish to incite in order to have people be controlled by their words to make people afraid of "otherness," of "big government." Insidiously then, the powers that be can become more and more wealthy while the little folks think they are going to someday win the penthouse. Actually the move is downward to the poorhouse *sans* any safety net. All the while, the powers that be continue to degrade the earth so that eventually it's not even going to be inhabitable for rich grandchildren. They may inherit money, but the earth is another matter. The Midas touch, you might say.

PENTHOUSE, POORHOUSE, PLUTOCRACY (AKA PLUTONOMY)

Bill Moyers and others have sounded the alarm about the rise, not of the wounded feminine, unfortunately, but of the plutocracy. Plutocracy is defined as a system whereby wealth is controlled by a few. Citigroup, in its own document, "Revisiting Plutonomy: The Rich Getting Richer," refashioned plutocracy as "plutonomy." This paper boasts that "market friendly governments have allowed the rich to prosper ... and take an increasing share of income and wealth over the last twenty years ... particularly the top 1% of the United States ... but plutonomists have benefited disproportionately ... and are likely to get even wealthier ... because the dynamics of plutonomy are still intact." (Bill Moyers, *Progressive Magazine*, "The Rule of the Rich," February , 2011.) These are Citigroup's own words.

So the guy with the rickety car who claims support of Mitt Romney won't be getting the penthouse anytime soon. Whether it's called plutocracy or plutonomy, the effect is the same. The wealth is becoming more concentrated and the middle class is headed down the ladder to join the poor (*nouveau pauvre?*).

Not a woman of feminine principle, Ayn Rand gave capitalism its ideological fervor. No, she didn't invent the dirty underbelly of capitalism, but she did portray its narcissism as noble. It wasn't hard for all those testosterone-driven adolescent boys, now men, to romance her for her lack of altruism, and for her disgust for the common good. (Remember they take a blind eye to her stance on civil rights, woman's rights, and her atheism—it's just her metaphorical money they're after.)

Perhaps these guys are just using her for a cheap thrill. The Limbaughs, Norquists, the Adelsons, and Koch brothers—to name a few—hide behind her ideology—it gives their greed a cover of philosophical integrity. Perhaps they are all laughing on their way to their Cayman Island bank. *Atlas Shrugged, The Fountainhead,* who cares when its *laissez faire?*

An example of plutocracy in action was the Wisconsin governor, Scott Walker, going after the teachers and their unions. The Koch brothers dumped millions into Walker's fight just so he could take away their collective bargaining rights. The teachers wanted to retain their unions and to retain collective bargaining; they were willing to take pension and pay cuts. But for patriarchal plutocrats, that is not enough. Walker and the Koch brothers wanted to bust the unions. This is the death knell for the middle class who get coffins while the plutocrats fill their coffers.

I see us regressing to a Charles Dickens universe where the chasm between the haves and the have-nots widens into a gaping gorge. As it is, 1% of the population has 50% of the wealth in this country. Clearly, the way to cure the huge deficit, that came about from too many tax cuts and pointless and unending wars, is to tax the wealthy again. Feminine-principled Warren Buffett accepts this! Why can't the CEO's who make hundreds and hundreds of times more than their employees repent from their greed, become aligned with the feminine principle of care and connection, and pay more taxes. They won't be out on the streets, their houses won't be foreclosed. In fact, they will still own multiple mansions. They will never miss the money. Deficit solved and the wounded feminine principle rises!

BARGAINS—FAUSTIAN OR OTHERWISE?

I love to find a bargain. We all love a bargain—wanting the cheapest price, the best deal. Sometimes, however, we collude with the patriarchal powers that be when we shop for bargains not minding how these items got to be such a steal. Perhaps they are a steal. Perhaps the bargain is the devil's price to pay for foreign workers in a faraway sweatshop while the employees in the U.S. shipping warehouse are also laboring under grotesque conditions and with pittances for pay. Perhaps we too are selling our souls, on a continuum with the CEO who engorges himself or herself with a $60,000 per minute salary.

I was recently confronted with the fact that I was colluding with such powers that be when I discovered that the Amazon cheap books I bought were shipped from a demeaning workplace environment. What I did after that is return to buy books at my old haunt, the Chester County Book Company. Yes, I paid full price, but I could talk to the bookseller who has been there for years and who has always been a great help with any book selections I make. Imagine that, a face to face encounter with a merchant—human exchange. Unfortunately, as I write this, the bookstore is being forced to close, or at least become a much smaller venue. There are many local residents who are decrying the loss of this literary sanctuary. Maybe it will transform into a new vibrant entity. As it is, the store owner seems to have felt the anonymous Amazon swallowing them whole. Of course, things change. What does not change, what remains constant, is the need for connection and relationship in our worldly transactions.

I long for real human exchange when I buy something. I want to have a conversation with the butcher and know where the chicken clucked and the cow mooed! Did they have a decent life before they got sacrificed for me? (I want the McDonald's nursery rhyme farm, not the franchise.)

My mother had a little dress shop in my hometown. This is a two-pronged memory. On the one hand, I think her customers sometimes forgot Helen Luke's notion about how people who want something for nothing de-value the human exchange so, even in eye to eye dealings, we can have dishonesty. Before becoming the country of the credit card, people put things "on charge," that was noted in a ledger. They took the apparel and paid my mother "on time"—she hoped.

Unfortunately, there seemed to be a sentiment among some that my mother must have gotten her merchandise for free. Hence, "on time" too frequently became "never." Basically, these customers stole from my mother, somehow rationalizing that she must not have paid for it anyway. That was the shadow aspect of the store.

The bright aspect, the other prong of the story, was that I had a relationship with all the merchants in town. As early as age eight, I enjoyed going to Joe Cohen at the Men's Shop to buy Christmas gifts at a "10% discount." Or I would walk over to John Kenney, the florist, have a nice chat and buy an armload of snapdragons for a couple of quarters my uncle had given me the week before. (This was especially a

May ritual when little Catholic girls might set up a shrine to the Blessed Mother.) It was in the relationship of these exchanges that was especially memorable. Yes, I was just a kid; yet, I wanted an exchange where I was paying for something and I was in relation to someone.

Simple as they are, those transactions of a child are in keeping with the feminine principle of relationship in an exchange. Complex as it is, the plunder by the patriarchal plutocracy de-values the feminine principle. The result of this plutocracy, of managing money for a small elite of individuals has created our global financial crisis.

Furthermore, growth of the plutocracy to the detriment of the common-wealth is anathema to the rise of the wounded feminine. It is the antithesis of the feminine principle which honors relationship, connection, and fairness in commerce and trade.

Yet, despite plutocracy, we do have a fair trade movement to support companies and businesses where workers earn a living wage and where the workplace is "healthy" and safe. Meanwhile, I continue to search for connection with shopkeepers—whether they be at the grocery store, the clothing store, wherever. When the human aspect is demeaned, I feel off kilter. Ever shopped at a store where all the salespeople seem demoralized? I think often where there is a disconnect and such demoralization, it is because the corporate "store" does not treat its employees well. The corporations and companies that understand the brilliance of "treat your employees well and they will treat you customers well" are few and far between. Look for them, and when you find them, patronize them! Or perhaps, better yet, MATRONIZE them!

I have my own list that I'm happy to share.

BETRAYAL

Writing about the feminine principle and money is heart breaking. I am not being facetious. The wounded feminine is rising yet the plutocracy of patriarchy still has the power and the money and those in control do not want to share the sandbox—let alone the toys in it.

In *Betrayal of the American Dream*, by Donald L. Barlett and James B. Steele, I highlight practically every word using, of course, my Kindle Fire, most likely made in China and shipped to my door by some Amazon awful warehouse. (Yes, I admit that I am part of the problem.) Perhaps the only company responsible to its employees in the process of my purchase was the UPS or FedEx that made the delivery. I think those drivers are making a decent wage and corporations have yet to figure out how to outsource them. Little balloon airdrops from Asia perhaps? Anyway, I could no more succinctly or thoroughly convey to the reader about the plight of the middle class against a ruling plutocracy than these two former Philadelphia Inquirer reporters have.

They have outlined the destruction of the American dream of democracy and the middle class with every turn of the page, or swipe of the finger.

Most of us have read or heard bits and pieces of the various stories—and then we forget. But here is the complete map, the connect-the-dots of the plutocracy, all in one place.

Yes, we know about the Apple sweat shops in China and then we assume, because we now know, that something has been or will be done. Great, the Foxconn Corporation managing the sweatshops put up nets around the dorm windows to prevent workers jumping to their deaths. That move toward suicide prevention didn't do anything to change the workers' environment, the workplace that caused the desire to die in the first place. The horrific conditions persist.

What a juxtaposition of worlds to the one Apple originally created for its workers.

One former Apple employee, Bill Stamp, interviewed by Barlett and Steele, reports how there had been camaraderie and collaboration at Apple. In other words, where there had been the honoring of the feminine principle, came a regression to the patriarchal plutocracy's siren call for the bottom line. Wall Street demanded, not a creative and connected workplace where people made decent salaries and had a solid middle class life, but a bigger profit for its bottom line. Workers both in the U.S. and China be damned: In the U.S., damned to unemployment; in China, a work world reminiscent of a Charles Dickens' universe despite the high technology of its manufacturing. "SACOM [an acronym for Students and Scholars Against Corporate Misbehavior, a Hong Kong organization founded in 2005], the Hong Kong human rights group ... described working conditions at one Foxconn plant making iPhones ... [workers] endure excessive and forced overtime ... skip dinner ... work on unpaid overtime shifts... SACOM calls Foxconn's Apple workers 'iSlaves.'" (Barlett and Steele, p. 92)

SACOM noted that workers are exhausted, overworked and are verbally and physically abused by supervisors. As a result, the suicide rate among these workers is high. Furthermore, Apple workers labor to make products they can never hope to buy (Barlett and Steele, p. 96):

> One young worker lamented that he couldn't even dream of owning an iPad because it would 'cost two month's salary'—a far cry from the working conditions of the young Apple in its U.S. factories. Bill Stamp remembers a day early in his career when Apple, having asked workers to come in on a Saturday, gave everyone a new Mackintosh as a bonus for a job well done. ... How quickly it all changed—how the door to so much opportunity and a secure future [for U.S. employees] suddenly slammed shut when Apple began to sub-contract the making of its basic products and then shipped all the work to other countries.

While the American worker, such as Bill Stamp, suffered a great loss when Apple forsook America in search of other shores, Apple shares soared,

As for Apple, moving jobs around couldn't have worked out better. The corporation sometimes has more cash in its bank than the U.S. Treasury. In January, 2012, the company became the most valuable corporation on this planet—its stock was worth $42 billion. (p. 3)

And new CEO Tim Cook? In 2011, he garnered a compensation package of $380 million. How many factory workers' pay is that? Five thousand people—like the size of my hometown—according to Barlett and Steele.

Everything about plutocracy and money and, therefore, power in the hands of a few, smacks of patriarchal inflation. Unprincipled and with no balance of the feminine principle, where will this take us? Plutocracy has seeped into our governmental systems where money buys legislation and the legislators. It is not big government that we should worry about, it is, "do we have a government that is for all the people or just for the very high rollers?"

The privatization of America is now where money speaks and doors open to the moneyed insiders. Otherwise, you are an outsider. Ever go to the beach and discover all the mega-houses looking out upon the ocean. Every access road is a private drive and there is no place to park? Ah, yes, my state and federal tax dollars pay for that ocean front, especially when there is storm reclamation involved. So I subsidize the wealthy and have a hard time gaining access to a "public beach." The same occurs at certain lakes. You know, the lake is there but it is nigh on impossible to find access to it: Private Lane Pine Trail—to Private Lane Moosehead Drive.

Exclusivity is hierarchal and is supported in plutocracy. Inclusivity is the nature of the feminine principle. How many of us outsiders will it take to bring about the rise of the wounded feminine? Or perhaps there are some feminine principled insiders who will heed the clarion call of the wounded feminine! Warren Buffett? Bill and Melinda Gates? George Soros? Gore Vidal, who was himself a man of inherited wealth, noted that the concern for the common-wealth had to come from the moneyed ranks. Occupy Wall Street was and still is a movement among the 99% that is a profoundly important step to redressing the wrongs of the plutocracy and is a sign of the Rise of the Wounded Feminine. However the 99% needs support from those feminine principled people of wealth whose influence could bring even more vigor to the wounded feminine rising.

The Wounded Feminine Rises in a Grocery Store

This morning I took a break from writing and went into town to buy some things for a birthday celebration for my daughter's fiancé. I considered, as I was driving around doing errands, how I do enjoy taking care of others, feeding them and wanting to bring them joy. I think that is what the feminine principle is about. It isn't entirely altruistic because in doing for others there is satisfaction for self. Of course, one can overdo, to the detriment of self and self-care. Once again, it is about finding the balance between the "I" and the "We."

Even in the errands, I took pleasure in engaging with the salesclerks and cashiers. It seems easy to do here in this little Maine lake town, that's true. Nevertheless, I did have an especially enjoying, while brief, conversation with a young woman who obligingly inscribed the cake, deftly designing a cursive *Happy Birthday* within the circle of carrots. In our exchange, I remarked on her unique earrings and she related that she had bought them at a local store (Mexicali Blues) that sold fair trade merchandise. Here was a feminine-principled young woman. There was an immediate recognition that we are of like mind. I felt in this exchange the wounded feminine is indeed rising.

5

POLITICS AND THE FEMININE PRINCIPLE

~~~

There is one lesson I have learned that I hold above all others from my experience as a father, teacher, community organizer, and U.S. senator: We should never separate the lives we live from the words we speak. To me, the most important goal is to live a life consistent with the values I hold dear and to act on what I believe in. (Paul Wellstone)

Wealth has always been influential in politics. Many who have run for office, at least in U.S. history, have been wealthy themselves. The Rockefellers, the Roosevelts, the Kennedys, the Bush's, the Heinz's, the Romneys, are just a few of the moneyed political names in recent memory. And some of these wealthy politicians of the past, out of their own *noblesse oblige* contributed handily to the commonweal(th). Where would the U.S. have been during the depression without FDR, for example?

Yet today, the plutocrats who are not necessarily holding office are nevertheless running the show. Barlett and Steele consider that given plutocracy's grip on government and politics, democracy is dying. They are blunt in their urgent concerns (pp. 4-5):

> *For decades Washington and Wall Street have been system-atically rewriting the rules of the American economy to bene-fit the few at the expense of the many—putting in place poli-cies that have steadily dismantled the foundation of Amer-ica's middle class.*
>
> *The future looks bleak for all but the richest Americans if these policies don't change.*

POLITICS AND MONEY

The rich buy influence. As the divide between them and everyone else has grown since the early 1970's, the wealthy have poured more and more money into lobbying and politics in order to control the agenda. Now the "one percent" is plowing untold millions into political contributions and lobbying, and every effort to try to reduce the influence of money in politics has been rebuffed. With the Supreme Court's Citizens United ruling of January 21, 2010, the message was driven home that politics had become slavishly addicted to the big bucks of the moneyed class and that the ability of average Americans to influence elected officials would be overwhelmed by that money. Now, for a price, the elite will select the candidates and bankroll the campaigns, and few politicians will be able to afford to give up the corporate dollars.

Barlett and Steele warn us (p. xiv):

The ruling class is defined by its ability to move money beyond the reach of government supervision. This has been accomplished in various ways, but the most important is arguably the establishment of a belief that government has no business in business. This creed has no basis in fact and is widely disproved by the performance of other governments around the world. But not in America. Instead, we have created the world's newest financial aristocracy, a class that has successfully put itself beyond the reach of government constraint and can pretty much do whatever it wants in pursuit of its own personal gain.

It is not big government, but rather big money that is minding the store and stealing from its till. If democracy is practically dead, I think it can only be revived if the wounded feminine rises, as it must!

Plutocracy and greed are simply subsets of patriarchal lust for power and dominance. Honoring the feminine principle of relationship and connection is the only way to regain our ballast—and our ballot.

Meanwhile, however, there is a change back from the old guard that is taking the form of a cavalry charge against women (and all that they stand for). Yet, keep in mind that the war on women that is being waged by patriarchal forces goes beyond gender. The repressive push against women's reproductive rights and the dismissiveness by some politicians about the violence against women is rearing its ugly head again because women and the concomitant feminine principle go against the grain of patriarchy and plutocracy.

The murderer, Anders Breivik, spoke for far more than himself when, in his 1500 page manifesto, he decried women coming into equality with men. He blamed the development of women's rights for fomenting multiculturalism and diversity. And, for that, he is right, honoring the feminine and the feminine principle does imply equality for all, inclusiveness, human rights and multiculturalism.

Unfortunately, it appears that Breivik spoke what is in the hearts and minds of many a patriarch. Some are more subtle and most don't want to outright kill anyone. Yet Breivik's message does slide off their tongues on occasion. An example: Rush Limbaugh's calling student Sandra Fluke a slut after her testimony at a congressional hearing about contraception needing to be provided by health care insurance. Another example: Representative Akin claiming "legitimate rape" would rarely result in pregnancy. These deplorable remarks, while not murderous, are nevertheless derived from an ideology as societally sick as Breivik's. (And sometimes could actually provoke murderous impulses on the part of others with minds as twisted as Breivik's.)

"Women's" issues are traditionally associated with reproductive choice, health care access, domestic violence, equal pay, sexual harassment, children's welfare. When the "war on women" is waged, these are the issues at stake and they go beyond being about women. These issues are the warp and woof of society for both men and women.

Katha Pollitt, in a discussion with other women published in *In These Times*, August, 2012, responds to others in the group that the war on women is not necessarily backfiring. She says:

> *The Republicans go all out, and only get a piece of what they demand—but they usually get something, and they also move the debate more to their side, so I would say the War on Women is going well. The Paycheck Fairness Act is dead, the Violent Against Women Act has to be reconciled between Senate and House, abortion restrictions are rampant, birth control is harder for poor women to get in some states. And the Republican war on "government workers"—mostly teachers—has been devastating for women.*

Despite these devastating blows to women's rights, Susan J. Douglas, at age 62, notes "... my generation needs to remind younger women that while challenging patriarchy is hard and often dispiriting work, speaking truth to power is, in fact, fun."

So, with that, let the fun begin!

At least now, the real sexist shadow of politics and the media is being seen outright. Not that crimes don't occur in broad daylight with witnesses watching either apathetically or helplessly. However, with abhorrent attitudes so shamelessly being stated, we can hope that there is a critical mass of us people, both men and women, to push back for the rise of the wounded feminine. We are lost if this does not happen.

Yet if we become demoralized, we are lost as well. So speaking truth to power requires playfulness so that we can have fun knocking plutocrats and patriarchal politicians (be they male or female) off their pedestals.

NAME THOSE PLUTOCRATS AND PATRIARCHAL POLITICIANS

To play at this, we need to know who the other team is. I resist calling them enemies or opponents because I want to consider their humanity even if they demean and subjugate mine. Relationship and connection is what we want to achieve in the end. I want to play on my humanitarian terms, not theirs. (I don't always succeed!)

The rich, first of all, have strong lobbies. Vast sums of money are spent in Washington to rewrite public policy in their favor. Barlett and Steele remark (pp. 18-19):

> *The rich were getting richer thanks to public policy. Their greatest victory—one that would aggravate the nation's deficit and substantially widen the gulf that separated them from everyone else—was lobbying Congress to rewrite the tax code in their favor. Since the 1980's, with a few exceptions, the tax rate of the very rich has gone straight down and now bears no resemblance to the rate during the years when America as a whole prospered. ... In addition ... Congress in 2003 reduced the tax on income from corporate dividends,*

one of the key income streams for the very wealthy that signif-
icantly benefits only about 2 percent of the taxpayers.

Furthermore, the lobby push is to have Congress eliminate the capital gains tax on sales of stock and assets. When Republican Newt Gingrich was campaigning for the 2012 presidency, according to Barlett and Steele, he spoke for many of the elite (p. 19):

> *... when he proposed doing away with the capital gains tax, ostensibly to spur investment in America. Eliminating that tax would deepen the income and wealth gap and do nothing to create jobs in America. But that's okay with the folks that make the rules ... inequity is a sensible price to pay for the greater profit on the sale of, well, equities.*

Writing about the wealthy gets personal. I admit it, so I am going to give voice to my story. This is where I lose my high road humanitarianism and do see the rich who rule as opponent. My own experience from my past and present rises up to greet me.

First, My Past. When I was a child my father was a guild (union) member who worked as a proofreader for the Philadelphia Inquirer. This was the job he landed after his own small town newspaper burnt to the ground in 1943. His business ran on barter and he had no renter's insurance. On the other hand, my mother's younger brother came home from World War II and went back to school on the GI bill and built his house on a government mortgage, only to turn around and demean my father in the 1950's for being a union man.

Once my golden boy uncle started to make money, he eschewed his working class background—his own father was a crane operator in a steel mill. Now that he was climbing the corporate ladder, unions were something to bust.

I argued against his comments even as a nine-year-old. Later I argued with him about his castigating remarks about the poor of Rio de Janiero. He was headed to be a vice president of ITT and while working as an efficiency expert (i.e., fire people) in Rio, he bemoaned the fact that the people of the barrios had such a good view, while his view was blighted by having to see their poverty. Needless to say, I carry my patriarchal uncle complex within. I too like nice things but his condescending attitude forever irritated me. The rest of the family cow-towed to him while I seethed. And he was so slick with words; he could put a person down before they even knew what hit them.

I suppose, in part, I feel the need to give voice to my story to right the wrongs of this relative whom I have projected onto many a patriarchal politician (for example, when I watch Bush or Romney smirk) that is forever in my craw. Yet I have internalized my uncle just as the daughter of a sexual abusing father might internalize her father. They are disturbing (all the while, outwardly charming and handsome) and yet there is a part of them that has become ingrained within. Indeed also, the genetic connection is there. And yes, of course, while I write this at a lake cottage that I rent, I would like to be moneyed enough to own it. We all want what money can buy. Not so unlike the guy with the Romney sticker am I.

And Now ... My present experience is the fact of my work. My earnings have not risen in years; nor have my husband's. It is not that I work less, but I get paid less. I am self-employed and partly rely on income from insurance companies. For one, Medicare has reduced its pay rate to psychologists over the years. And another insurance company reduced their pay rate of twenty years ago then raised it back to that 1990's rate only when I questioned the administrator whether her pay had been reduced over the last twenty years. While I am not even getting cost of living raises, I am certain the high level manager and the CEO's of this insurance company and all others are not simply making out like bandits—they are bandits.

And Medicare? It gets stymied in Congress every year so that payments for mental health services provided by psychologists are losing ground.

DAUGHTERS OF PATRIARCHAL POLITICS

The stereotype of women is that they align themselves with healthcare and with the care and welfare of the family. For some women (Republicans are noted here) the stereotype has morphed into being about "pro-life." (That is, anti-abortion, since life after birth is rarely considered a worthy concern for these politicians. Health, education, and welfare goes by the wayside once born.) Marjorie Dannenfelser is president of the Susan B. Anthony List (if only the suffragette herself could come back to life!), a fund-raising organization for anti-abortion female candidates. She apparently has raised millions in support of candidates such as Nikki Haley, Carly Fiorina, and Meg Whitman.

I read about Dannenfelser in a *Philadelphia Inquirer* column by Kevin Ferris. This is my journal entry of June 13, 2010:

SUNDAY, JUNE 13, 2010

Today, I read Kevin Ferris' commentary in the Inquirer. I used to send Kevin my community commentaries back in the days when he was a liberal. I met him at a Labor Day crab fest, given by my friend, Fawn Vrazo, who was his colleague at the paper. We talked about Quaker schools, his kids, my kids. Kevin is a changeling! Now he is a conservative who has not lost his writing skills.

This particular Sunday, he compares YOW—the Year of the Woman, 1992, with the year 2010's YOW. Patricia Ireland, president of NOW proclaimed then, "In this season of discontent, it will be women who can transform the national rage and demoralization into hope." His read, of course, is that these words from an earlier liberal would now be voiced by latter day conservative, Republican women. Carly Fiorina, Meg Whitman, Sarah Palin, Nikki Haley, to name some.

The shoulders that these conservative women stand upon are shuddering. They belong to the women who espoused "liberal" causes and cried out for equality for women. How quickly these new women forget all the tears and toil of the pioneers before them. Are they like rebellious adolescents who don't want to listen to Mama's wisdom? Or are they so taken in by patriarchy that they can't see how they have sold their hearts and souls to the status quo that so desperately needs to change? These women, driven as they are by negative animus, are not our hope and they are not about change and transformation to a new order. They are keeping the hierarchy-patriarchy intact. Oh, they do well personally. But then their model Ayn Rand only cared about the personal, not the common good.

I want to cry out, Wake up, World, Stop shooting yourself in the foot! Do you not see that such women (and men) care little about best interest, only themselves? There are people of power who also have heart. These are not it. The women of power who also have loving hearts, not just for their kith and kin, but to see everyone as part of an "us" not a "them," are the women we want to see in politics.

THE POLITICS OF HEALTH CARE

The plutocracy has propagandized that the private market is the way to have health care. Barlett and Steele in *Critical Condition: How Health Care in America Became Big Business—and Bad Medicine* (2004) documented how the market failed to deliver "quality healthcare to everyone at an affordable price." (*The Betrayal of the American Dream*)

Atal Gawande, M.D., echoes their refrain. In 2009, at a conference of state leaders of the American Psychological Association, Gawande warned that the uninsured are a bellwether of suffering and that the number one cause of bankruptcy in the U.S. is due to health care costs. A cancer surgeon himself, he noted that to provide insurance to the uninsured would reduce both the cancer rate and mental illness. To be a stronger country, he believes, the government must recognize the need for health care insurance for all. He optimistically said that when the recalcitrant (my word for his word: Republicans) realize that economic interests suffer when the health of the citizens suffer perhaps they'll get the message. This line of thought is akin to how labor leader Cesar Chavez championed the rights of the migrant workers picking grapes. These workers were getting poisoned and sick from the pesticides that were being sprayed. Nobody cared that the workers were becoming ill. Then Chavez said, the insecticide residue is on the food you eat and you'll be sick too. Then the alarm bells rang, because the consumers cared. Where altruism fails, selfishness that delivers to the common good as well will do.

But the message hasn't come home to roost yet, because even though Obama's health care bill has passed, there are hollers from the right to repeal it. Barlett and Steele are incredulous (p. xviii):

> *[Even though] the private market has failed, ... Obama's health care bill still leaves most of the power over the health industry in the hands of private insurers. It is a mark of how effectively the ruling class's propaganda machine has become in framing the debate in America that this relatively benign piece of legislation would be portrayed as a triumph of "socialism." ... We have become a plutocracy in which the few enact programs that promote their narrow interest at the expense of many.*

The Balance of the Feminine and the Masculine

Hanna Rosin (in the July-August, 2010 issue of *The Atlantic* magazine) wrote an article entitled "The End of Men: How Women Are Taking Control of Everything." I sighed and wondered, what women? Rosin noted that even patriarchal South Korea has seen a sea change in attitudes towards women since the 1970's and 1980's when the government, wanting to bolster industrial and economic growth, supported women's efforts to join the work force.

I am reminded, however, of Rosie, the Riveter. Remember how in World War II women were needed in the factories because the men were fighting overseas? When the men came marching home, the women were expected to march out of the workforce and become high-heeled housewives buying 1950's appliances.

Keep this reminiscence on the back burner of your mind even if Rosin doesn't. In Korea now, having a son is no longer as paramount as it had been in women's lives. By 2003, that aspiration, she claims, has been all but extinguished. Monica Das Gupta, a demographer and Asia expert at the World Bank, for support, states that male preference for a child in South Korea is over (World Bank Policy Research Working Paper No. 4373, 10/7/2007, "Why is son preference declining in South Korea? The role of development and public policy, and the implications for China and India").

Supposedly, this shift is occurring in countries such as India and China also. A hybrid of Marlboro man and biologist, lab-coated cowboy Ronald J. Ericsson in the 1970's discovered a method of separating sperm that carried the Y chromosome from those that carried the X. As Rosin reports, he believed at the time that this would provide parents a choice regarding the sex of their child. He expected that the winner would be the Y—that is, the chromosome that determines maleness.

To his surprise, Americans, if given the choice, slightly preferred girls. Now that Ericcson has a feisty and talented young adult granddaughter who seems to fit into his labcoat as well as his cowboy boots, he rides a new horse: "... those females are going to leaves us males in the dust."

Rosin considers we may be on the last gasp of a dying age; and, while I agree about that, the patriarchy is not giving up without a fight. The rise of the wounded feminine is occurring. But it is not about women becoming daughters of the patriarchy themselves and claiming "women have made it."

However, Rosin does note how "near the top of the jobs pyramid ... the march of women stalls. Prominent female CEO's, past and present, are so rare they count as minor celebrities ... the accomplishment is considered so extraordinary that Whitman and Fiorina are using it as the basis for their political campaigns."

Ay, and there is the rub. Just because it is a woman CEO or a female politician does not mean we have had a change of patriarchal guard.

Carly Fiorina, although she left Hewlett-Packard with millions ($21.4 million in cash to Fiorina plus stock and pension benefits worth another $19 million), she was asked to resign after practically destroying the reputation of what had been a very reputable company, which was also very mindful of and responsible to its employees before her arrival!

I don't know which is more detrimental to the feminine principle: the male patriarch or the female rendition of patriarchy. I repeat my refrain: The rise of the wounded feminine and the honoring of the feminine principle goes beyond gender. Both women and men of heart have much to contribute to the collaborative transformation of the world to a kinder place.

Despite Rosin's glibly optimistic musings about couples wanting daughters, according to Mara Hvistendahl, Rosin's data are skewed. In *Unnatural Selection: Choosing Boys Over Girls, and the Consequences of a World Full of Men*, Hvisten-dahl, to Rosin's assertion that the "traditional order has been upended," replies (pp. 256-257):

In fact the traditional order has only been upended in the United States, where a shift in gender preferences barely makes a dent in the global imbalance. And examining why American parents want girls suggests that in one crucial way things have not changed all that much. ...

Americans who select for sex are intent on having girls because of preconceived notions of how a girl will turn out. Bioethicist Dena S. Davis writes that people who take pains to get a child of a certain sex "don't want just the right chro-mosomes and the attendant anatomical characteristics, they want a set of characteristics that go with 'girlness' or 'boy-

ness.' ... If parents want a girl badly enough to go to all the trouble of sperm sorting and artificial insemination, they are likely to make it more difficult for the actual child to resist their expectations and follow her own bent." In that sense American parents seeking a girl are no different from the Indian couple that selects for a son with the expectation he will turn into an upstanding heir. "It's not like [parents in the developing world] who are doing this thing are somehow weird," says Marcy Darnovsky, directory of the Center for Genetics and Society, a Berkeley NGO focused on human genetic and reproductive technologies. "We're doing it, too. So let's look in the mirror, folks."

Sex selection is about preconceived (!) notions about why a child needs to be a boy or a girl. The fact that Americans may prefer girls is no more justifiable than Asian or Eastern European couples believing boys are better. The ethics of sex selection, whatever it be, for boy or girl babies, is side-stepped.

Hvistendahl disagrees with both Das Gupta and Rosin. Where Das Gupta saw an "incipient turnaround in the phenomenon of missing girls in Asia" (in Hvistendahl, p. 298), Hvistendahl notes no such thing. Travelling to South Korea to witness this "new wave of gender equality" (p. 234), she found little change. And asking sociologist Whasoon Byun whether government policy had led to an improvement in the status of women, Byun laughs and says "that the notion that Korean women are significantly better off than they were ten or twenty years ago must have been put in ... [Hvistendahl's] head by a man" (p. 235).

In the Caucasus, Eastern Europe, China, India, South and East Asia—even parts of the U.S.—there is a gender imbalance of boys to girls. When population control in developing nations was pushed by the West, "the unintended consequence" (Hvistendahl re-defines that "as any means to an end") was sex selection. If a family can only have one child, the woman's belief is that it needs to be a son. Regardless of the man's influence, the mother often feels, why bring a girl into a man's world to be a second class inhabitant of it.

The imbalance of 112 to 120 boys per 100 girls in Asian populations has far flung consequences, leading to bride-buying, sex trafficking, and a rise in crime. Historically, population excesses of males appears to lead to violence and instability.

With violence and aggression there is a gender difference due to amounts of testosterone. Everyone has the hormone but men, of course, have a preponderance of it in comparison to women. Testosterone in and of itself does not cause human violence, but it can elevate aggressive tendencies in certain environments. This is what, according to Hvistendahl, scientists term a "facilitative effect."

Scientists are now finding that a reversal to the facilitative effect of testosterone is marriage and children. In a longitudinal study of Air Force veterans it was found that testosterone levels dropped when these men married and increased with divorce (Mazur and Michalek).

I would add, this is where the feminine principle comes into play. In marriage and family there is relationship and connection and support.

Actually with the birth of infants, another hormone, oxytocin, is not only produced in the mother but in the father as well. Some call this the love hormone, I'd like to dub it the feminine principle hormone instead.

6

THE LARSSON TRILOGY

*No matter what fate befalls us—even a very dark one—we
will be safe if the feminine can hold. (Robert Johnson)*

Given that my sense of the rise of the wounded feminine
crystallized when heroine Lisbeth Salander's hand rose
from the grave at the end of the Swedish film, *The Girl Who
Played with Fire*, I am indebted to feminine principled Stieg
Larsson for having written this trilogy. Here, he, in his sto-
ries, *The Girl with the Dragon Tattoo* (Swedish title: *Men Who
Hate Women*), *The Girl Who Played with Fire*, and *The Girl
Who Kicked the Hornet's Nest*, call for a separate chapter.

I think he described in fiction what are the complicated
facts of patriarchy—how money, power, and old school politics meld with a hatred of women, the feminine principle,
and all things "other"—many times, other than white
"Christian" male, basically. We live in a cultural context.

So isn't it interesting that Stieg Larsson's trilogy of novels has been translated from Swedish and has been published in more than forty countries. It would appear that these tales of heroine Lisbeth Salander and investigative journalist Mikael Blomkvist are more than fleeting crime novels and are a tapping into what Carl Jung would call our collective unconsciousness?

And perhaps the collective at some level is beginning to attend to the message that Larsson conveys about men and a decaying patriarchal system and about women who have been subjected to emotional and physical violence for centuries.

The psychology of Carl Jung can help us understand Larsson's cast of characters psychodynamically and give light to the collective dysfunction that the novels portray.

I believe that Larsson provokes us to consider that the wounded feminine, having been buried and suppressed, is now rising in new form.

Recently, I picked up the Solstickan matchbox from Sweden and remembered why and when I bought a whole raft of these. Pictured on the tiny box of wooden matches is a little child walking under a bright red-orange sun: Solstickan says the box. So joyous an illustration. And I thought these matchboxes would be a clever way to remember our summer vacation in Sweden—the subway's richly colored murals on the tunnel's rocky underground, the bicycling on Faro, the boat ride through the archipelago out of Stockholm, the cabin by the river and our canoe paddling like hell against the rising wind (perhaps that was telling me something there). I remember Sweden being quiet and peaceful, yet like the wind on the river there was a glimmer of another story to be told.

I met a Swedish colleague, family therapist-psychologist who refrained from giving me her address and preferred instead to meet at a coffee shop near my hotel. When we met to discuss a new therapy technique in which we had both been trained—ETT (Emotional Transformation Therapy)—she related to me that she had been under some police protection because she worked with refugee women who were breaking away from their abusive husbands, families, whomever. So not only were these young women in danger of recrimination but so was she. That is, her life too may have been in danger.

At the time, although aghast at her personal story, I didn't see it beyond its particular reference to her and her clients. I didn't see the larger context, and so, though recalling her and her story, during our vacation (and thereafter), I continued to enjoy the seeming peace of the people and the solitude of the landscapes of Sweden.

That is until I see the Solstickan matchbox again, three years later in the movie rendition of Stieg Larsson's "The Girl Who Played with Fire" and "Girl with the Dragon Tattoo." The matchbox now has taken on a whole reversed valence. A symbol perhaps, of the fierce and fiery rage of Lisbeth, the female protagonist of the Larsson trilogy. Lisbeth, who with the aid of a match, sets her sadistically abusive father on fire. The child of the matchbox no longer representing an innocent under the sun but a soul wounded by malevolent males.

Solstickan matchbox. (Photo by the author)

The once innocuous matchbox startled me into recalling the unsettling conversation with the Swedish colleague about threats upon her own life as she sought protection for the young women in her care.

Interestingly, Stieg Larsson's first novel of the trilogy, while known to us as *The Girl with the Dragon Tattoo*, was originally titled *Men Who Hate Women* in Swedish.

And so, why I address these books (now also in movies) here is that I believe they are far more than entertainment.

There is, I think, a profound significance that they appear now, to capture the psyches of so many of us.

Briefly, the trilogy intertwines the lives of the characters, Lisbeth Salander and Mikael Blomkvist. Lisbeth is a young woman who witnessed the brutal abuse of her mother by her father, and was then brutally abused herself over the years by so called professionals and caretakers. However, she used her brilliant mind and her cunning to face traumatic events with a solitary sense of "I will not be a victim." Blomkvist is the investigative reporter whose life becomes entangled with hers. Together they solve in the first book, a mystery disappearance of a young woman of a wealthy business family, only to discover sexual abuse within the family, along with vicious hate crimes against many women.

Abuse of women is not "over there," somewhere or nowhere—"only a movie."

Domestic violence, rape, sexual abuse remain in all societies to one degree or another. Stieg Larsson's novels and the movie versions thereof are graphic and difficult, but somehow also compelling because their portrayal of violence against women is not gratuitous.

There has been both a fear and a putdown of women for thousands of years with the rise of patriarchy. Just as in the dialectic of master and slave, neither men nor women win in patriarchy. When we denigrate a people by nationality, gender, religion, socio-economic class, we eventually denigrate ourselves. And so the patriarchy, in its creating a hierarchical structure based on power, greed, wealth, material resources, territory—in the end subsumes itself. Patriarchy, in its denial of the feminine principle (within all of us) cannot sustain itself forever.

I think Stieg Larsson got this. His novels are not simple escapism/crime fiction. I believe he had set out to influence—perhaps even unbeknownst to him—the collective psyche to see the elephant in the living room. That is, that the abuse of women, the rape of the feminine, was not only to individual women (millions though they are) but that there is a global rape created by a patriarchal, hierarchical perspective which cannot abide the rising feminine.

QUICK VISITS TO EACH BOOK

THE GIRL WITH THE DRAGON TATTOO
(SWEDISH TITLE: MEN WHO HATE WOMEN)

Here we are introduced to Lisbeth Salander, a petite young woman who was considered a ward of the state and psychologically incompetent. In the first book (and movie), we don't yet know why, but we later find out that she was declared incompetent after her mother was permanently brain damaged and hospitalized (due to Lisbeth's father), and after Lisbeth hurled a Molotov cocktail at her father. Lisbeth herself is then brutalized in the psychiatric hospital by Dr. Teleborian. Her first guardian after that horror is Holger Palmgren, a wise elder, who is kind to her. When Palmgren becomes ill, she is remanded to Nils Bjurman, who also brutalizes her.

In the midst of the violence done to her by Bjurman, we see her as a computer genius hacker, a woman with a brilliant mind and an eidetic memory. She works for Milton

Secruity, whose owner Dragan Armansky also shows concern for her.

Lisbeth's life crosses with Mikael Blomkvist because she is investigating him for Milton Security. While Blomkvist's own investigation of Swedish billionaire industrialist Hans-Erik Wennerstrom lands him in jail after losing a libel suit, Henrick Vanger, another industrialist, is planning to hire him for a personal assignment. Vanger's enlistment of Milton Security to do the vetting of his background is the beginning of Lisbeth's connection to Mikael.

After learning that he has been sentenced to jail for three months, Mikael meets Vanger and finds that his assignment is to solve the disappearance of Vanger's great niece, Harriet. Vanger assumes that a family member murdered her 40 years ago.

When Mikael discovers that Lisbeth has hacked into his computer, he enlists her help in cracking the "cold case" of Harriet's disappearance.

What ensues is a discovery of sexual abuse in the family that devolves into vicious hate crimes against women. It is Lisbeth's skill and Mikael's determination that unveils the terrifying mystery. Although Vanger had lured Mikael to solve the family mystery by hope of also nailing Wennerstrom, his information is scant. It is Lisbeth who discovers that Wennerstrom's dealings are criminal beyond what Mikael had reported earlier. With her help, his new expose destroys Wennerstrom and his investigative magazine Millennium is not only vindicated but hurled into national prominence.

THE GIRL WHO PLAYED WITH FIRE

In *The Girl Who Played With Fire*, Mikael Blomkvist, investigative journalist and part owner of Millennium magazine, encounters a young journalist named Dag Svensson and his companion, Mia Johannson. Both have done significant research regarding sex trafficking: a meticulously researched thesis about sex trafficking in Sweden and those in high office who abuse underage girls. Blomkvist immediately throws himself into the investigation.

Mikael Blomkvist has had no contact with Lisbeth Salander since they risked their lives on a hunt for a serial killer a year earlier (see *The Girl with the Dragon Tattoo*). Unknown to Blomkvist, however, Salander has been surveilling him via his computer's hard drive, which she has linked to and is monitoring from her vast new apartment (which no one knows the address to).

Armed with a photographic memory and focused on seeking out and punishing "men who hate women," Salander is drawn to the investigation on Blomkvist's computer. So while Blomkvist and his fellow journalists research the sex industry, Lisbeth—spurred on by the case studies of child prostitution she finds on Blomkvist's computer—becomes involved. She goes to visit Svensson and Johannson in order to help them; she instead gets blamed for their murders, as well as for the murder of her abusive guardian, Nils Bjurman, who might know more about Zala, the mysterious name that pops up wherever the words "sex trafficking" are, than she even dared to think.

It is in this second novel that Lisbeth confronts her

father who is at the dark core of the story. Meanwhile, she gets labeled by tabloids and certain bigoted and misogynist detectives as a lesbian, and S&M Satanist.

THE GIRL WHO KICKED THE HORNET'S NEST
(SWEDISH TITLE: THE AIR CASTLE THAT EXPLODED)

It must be noted here that the film depiction of this novel goes far afield from the book's characterization of Erika Berger, the editor of Millennium, the investigative journal central to the trilogy. (It seems that the patriarchy snuck in here.) She is a close friend and sometime lover of Mikael who, in the film, appears timid and collapsed in the face of sexual and violent threats. In Larsson's novel, she remains, as ever, steadfast in her determination to stand and fight against any violence, whether directed towards herself or anyone else. Also in the novel she leaves Millennium to go to the mainstream media for a while—and that is where threats to her life arise.

I believe that Larsson would be hard pressed to approve of the film's rendering of Erika Berger because it is so aberrant from his continual message about women as enduring against all odds and not collapsing into the patriarchal violence that undergirds society's ills.

Briefly, the story begins with Lisbeth lying in critical condition, bullet wound to head, having been shot and buried alive by her father in the second novel. Down the hall from her room lies her father, the evil Zalachenko, also wounded. With the help of kind Dr. Johansson, a man not of the patriarchy, Lisbeth will survive as long as her father does not have the chance to again do otherwise.

While it is Zalachenko who should be facing trial, instead it is Lisbeth who will be going to trial for three murders. Mikael engages his sister Annika to become Lisbeth's defense attorney (interestingly, in the movie, she is pregnant).

In this novel, proving of her own innocence, Lisbeth also shows how those in authority, such as Nils Bjurman and Dr. Teleborian, have been the perpetrators of evils against women.

An aging and dying cabal of men (a secret subset, the Section, of the government's Sapo, secret police) kill each other off to keep their illegal and immoral secrets safe.

WHO IS STIEG LARSSON?

How is it that an unknown Swedish journalist would take on the avocation of writing lengthy and complicated crime novels in which an abused young woman becomes the heroine and whose cohort is an investigative journalist?

Actually there may be some slim parallels between Stieg Larsson and the journalist Mikael Blomkvist of his novels. Larsson himself established an investigative journal, *Expo*, after eight people were murdered in Sweden by Neo-Nazis. In the novels, Blomkvist is editor of the investigative journal *Millennium:* And Larsson himself was no stranger to right wing death threats and violence due to his reporting.

In fact, Larsson and his longtime partner Eva Gabrielsson never married so that their address and other information would not become public knowledge. A bittersweet and tragic relief to Eva Gabrielsson was that Larsson died suddenly of a heart attack rather than having been gunned down by white supremacists. Also sadly, Gabrielson reports that Larsson was working on the fourth of what was to be ten books. She also highlights what were traumatic events in Larsson's history. A most important influence in Larsson's life was that, when he was fifteen, he witnessed a gang rape, in which he knew both the perpetrators and the victim and failed to intervene. The girl's name was Lisbeth. From that time on, he wanted to expose violence and abuse of women. In an interview with Rachel Cooke from *The Observer* (February 21, 2010), Larsson's lifelong companion, Eva Gabrielsson, notes, "Stieg's feminism—the driving force of the books—was so important. Partly this was thanks to his upbringing, to his closeness to his grandmother. But it's also that, when he was fourteen or fifteen, he was witness to a gang-rape committed by his so-called friends. This is the key thing. For him, the fight against violence against women was personal."

Gabrielsson, in the same interview, makes the connection between Stieg Larsson's investigative journalism and the journalist Björn Söderberg, who was murdered in his suburban Stockholm home by Neo-Nazis in October, 1999. His investigations exposed Nazism and racism. We may think that's Nordic Sweden, not us. But in this country, the Southern Poverty Law Center reports that white supremacist, and other, hate groups are on the rise.

Larsson's real life history intertwined with his fiction writing to now inform the collective. Carl Jung would say that the acts of active imagination, whether they are our individual interactions with our own dreams, or they are the creations of artists or writers, move us to a transformation of consciousness. Active imagination is a way to give voice to the unconscious sides of the personality unseen (especially anima/animus and the shadow). Even when the end products are not interpreted, for example, with the Larsson trilogy, something happens between the creator and the creation that makes way for a transformation of consciousness.

My point here is that even if Larsson was not totally aware of all that he was bringing forward from the collective unconscious to consciousness, it is happening anyway. And that the creator, the writer, the poet, the artist, then can help us move to greater consciousness as well.

The Trilogy and the Rise of the Wounded Feminine

In an earlier chapter, we defined *anima* and *animus*. Rudimentarily put, *anima* and *animus* are soul qualities: they are the contra-sexual soul aspects of man and woman. A woman contains within, *animus*, masculine logos qualities; a man contains, with *anima*, feminine soul qualities or *eros*.

In negative form, the *anima* in a man manifests in irrational moods and emotions; the negative *animus* of a woman is displayed in sweeping generalizations and imperatives. The positive *animus* is courageous, creative, independent, wise. The positive *anima* of a man is inspired, emotionally connected, animated.

We see in the characters of Lisbeth and Mikael the *animus* and *anima* at play. Mikael is receptive, waiting, empathetic. Lisbeth is logical and focused, and she also has internalized the *animus* of her first guardian, Palmgren, who taught her always to weigh the consequences of any action.

Yet her half-brother, Niedermann, who appears in the second and third novels, does not carry his *anima* soul, the feminine, in its positive valence. Her half-brother, in what he displays to the world, is hyper-masculine. He is huge and literally feeling no pain due to his own neural disease. Yet we are reminded that in terms of a man's *anima*, all that is absent in outer expression will be found within (C. G. Jung, CW 6, par. 804):

> *The tyrant tormented by bad dreams, gloomy forebodings, and inner fears is a typical figure. Outwardly ruthless, harsh, and unapproachable, he jumps inwardly at every shadow, is at the mercy of every mood, as though he were the feeblest and most impressionable of men. Thus his anima contains all those fallible human qualities his persona lacks. If the persona is intellectual, the anima will certainly be sentimental.*

And we see Niedermann run from his own shadow, and from noises in the night. It is not from guilty conscience of having murdered and maimed so many, but from this loss of *anima* soul within that creates the fearful monster.

Perhaps Niedermann is the hyperbole of the patriarch who fears change and the unknown.

Whenever we read books or view movies, plays, TV shows, we are encountering archetypes, as psychologically defined by Carl Jung: "... [one] archetype is an image of instinct [and] is a spiritual goal toward which the whole nature of man strives; it is the sea to which all rivers wend their way, the prize which the hero wrests from the fight with the dragon" (C.G. Jung, CW 6, par. 415).

Archetypes are inherent to the human psyche; they can't be known directly but arise universally in all cultures. Examples of archetypal symbols: hero, water of life, wise old man, nourishing mother, devouring mother.. . We all know the archetypes of both Superman and Wonder Woman.

ARCHETYPES

Encountering an archetype shows us that our individual themes and problems are also themes of humanity and make them universal (adapted from Chalquist).

Lisbeth is an archetypal perhaps sometimes Kali figure who carries her inner masculine, animus soul. She is powerful, athletic and in her computer hacker skills, her interest in higher mathematics, her eidetic memory she carries the logos of animus. She appears antisocial, it is true, but that to my mind is the result of having witnessed the violence of her father against her mother, and her having been brutalized herself by the psychiatrist, Dr. Teleborian and by her second guardian, Nils Bjurman; or perhaps it is as the Jungians Marie Louise van Franz and Helen Luke note: the heroine must withdraw from the world in introversion, "where she must go apart and endure the suffering of silent waiting for the time of her deliverance" (Luke, p. 23). Even in the midst of torment, Lisbeth does not succumb to what Jung would term *abaissement du niveau mental*, which he described as a "loss of soul." She does not lose her *animus* soul but instead becomes a warrior to right the injustices done not only to herself and her mother but also to other women as well.

IDENTIFICATION AND OVER-IDENTIFICATION (INFLATION) WITH ARCHETYPES (ARCHETYPE AND ACTOR)

It is dangerous for any of us to over-identify with an archetype, such as "goddess," "god," "demon," "lover," whatever. The character Lisbeth is played by Noomi Rapace, and in an interview heard on National Public Radio, she noted that at the end of production of the last movie, she did not at first partake in the champagne festivities. She instead went to the bathroom and retched and shook. I would say that, from the Jungian perspective, she was purging herself of identification with the archetype. When we over-identify with an archetype, we lose our sense of place in humanity. Noomi instinctively knew to let go of her identification with the archetypal character of Lisbeth. However, one could also say that Noomi was purging herself of the trauma history and rage carried in the character. Peter Levine describes shaking as the body's mechanism of release of trauma.

In an interview with Charlie Rose, Noomi Rapace calls Salander a beautiful survivor who fights for life. She is an underdog and is lonely but still turns her anger into strength even while feeling an alien and misfit. She refuses to play by the rules and expectations of the patriarchy. Noomi notes that she went deep inside herself to be true to the character and to Stieg Larsson. She saw Salander as wanting to live life and be free and was not sweet to suit you. Her sexuality was not to be defined.

Because Noomi Rapace went so inside her character she felt Lisbeth Salander helped her to be braver with her dark strong energy. While she was working on the films, she did note that for a time she felt everybody was against her. However, the other side of this was that Noomi understood that it is not necessary to be liked to be true to oneself. To disengage from the archetype she said "my body was throwing Lisbeth out of me."

COLLECTIVE UNCONSCIOUS

Jung went beyond the personal unconscious because he observed how often dreams and fantasies cannot be reduced to an individual's personal past experiences. I note here that why else would myths, fairy tales, and here the Larsson trilogy, capture a universal imagination.

A part of the collective unconscious is the concept/archetype of "the self." Because "the self" is an archetype, it is essentially unknowable. We see its manifestation in myths and legends—and, I would say, the heroic novels of Larsson. Jung says (C.G. Jung, CW 6, par. 790):

The self appears in dreams, myths, and fairytales in the figure of the "supraordinate personality," such as a king, hero, prophet, saviour, etc., or in the form of a totality symbol, such as the circle, square, quadratura circuli, cross, etc. When it represents a complexio oppositorum, a union of opposites, it can also appear as a united duality, in the form, for instance, of Tao as the interplay of yang and yin, or of the hostile brothers, or of the hero and his adversary (arch-enemy, dragon), Faust and Mephistopheles, etc. Empirically, therefore, the self appears as a play of light and shadow, although conceived as a totality and unity in which the opposites are united.

"The self" might appear as a vision of opposites, or of hero and adversary. So we read Larsson's novels and watch the screen adaptations meeting the archetype of self in the relationship of Mikael and Lisbeth.

My hunch is that if Larsson had been able to finish the ten books he had planned, we would have found psychological transformation in Lisbeth and Mikael, and their relationship. Would the world around them also evolve from its patriarchal oppression? Interestingly, Jung thought that the number ten was the number of high-level unity.

Supposedly, the fourth novel, unfinished, takes place in Canada. Lisbeth and Mikael are possibly searching for someone. Would Lisbeth's lost twin be living in Nova Scotia with Pema Chodron as a Buddhist nun meditating loving kindness?

SHADOW

Shadow can contain repressed desires, uncivilized impulses, immoral motives, resentments, childish fantasies—all that which one would rather disown. And so the disowning takes place as a projection on others. Projection is basically seeing in others what we are unconscious of in ourselves.

The brighter the persona, the darker the shadow. The persona inhibits the shadow from being known. The shadow is not always the dark underbelly of the personality. It may also have a positive valence—and may contain moral qualities and abilities that have been repressed.

Lisbeth's persona looks like shadow to the so-called civilized people around her in *The Girl Who Kicked the Hornets' Nest*. She goes to court, not dressed in a simple chic suit, but with spiked hair, black and Goth to the hilt. She seems to be asking society to look at its own shadow, or perhaps it goes deeper than that. Helen Luke, in *The Way of Women*, talks about Simone Weil's notion of the soul's journey—that of its essential ingredients—is suffering social rejection (p. 21).

Nils Bjurman and Dr. Teleborian, meanwhile, present as the epitome of professional persona; meanwhile, their evil shadow lurks within.

WISE OLD MAN AS ARCHETYPE

Jung informs us in *The Phenomenology of the Spirit in Fairy-tales* (CW 9i, par. 398):

> *The figure of the wise old man can appear, not only in dreams*
> *but also in visionary meditation (or what we call "active*

imagination"), that . . . it takes over the role of a guru. The wise old man appears in dreams in the guise of a magician, doctor, priest, teacher, professor, grandfather, or any person possessing authority.

Palmgren, Lisbeth's first guardian, is a wise old man who supports the wounded feminine in the way he has, throughout the trilogy, been on her side . Vanger, the business mogul in The Girl With the Dragon Tattoo, in his wanting to reconcile the disappearance of his niece, also supports the wounded feminine and becomes a wise old man. Dragan Armansky, her employer, was also portrayed as a wise *animus* figure.

CONCLUSION OR TRANSFORMATION?

In the second novel, with a deer innocently grazing in the silent morning, Lisbeth literally digs herself out of the grave her father and brother have thrown her in. Rising from the earth, the wounded feminine claims her power. Note here the deer. The deer, according to Marija Gimbutas in *Language of the Goddess*, is the sacred animal of the birth-giving goddess of ancient times. While Stieg Larsson did not incorporate the deer in his novel, its appearance in the film seems synchronistic.

Larsson's Lisbeth depicted the young wounded feminine evolving from her abusive history to reclaim her power. Larsson's alter ego Blomkvist was the epitome of the new man—carrying his own gentle receptivity to meet the assertive feminine embodied in Lisbeth.

163

And where do Pippi Longstocking and Kalli Blomqvist and Solstickan fit in?[1] Mikael and Lisbeth continually referred to each other as the mystery story heroes of their childhood. Lisbeth called her flat Villakula as did Pippi call her home. Perhaps the inner child is becoming a symbol of transformation. Project on this how you like.

Fiction can be like a parable. Some people get the message. Others simply twist the message into some literal narrow meaning. My hunch, however, is that there's got to be something afoot in the collective mind (interesting image—foot in mind) that prompts Larsson's trilogy to be as ubiquitous as a Sarah Palin pun. And there the similarity stops—cold as a snowy day in Sweden.

Goddess Pele I believe would want Larsson's spirit to continue the quest to wrest the wounded feminine from the death grasp of the patriarchy.

Hopefully a Jungian perspective can help midwife a birthing of a new consciousness in which the feminine principle is honored in both men and women.

1. Note that Solstickan is a Swedish charity founded in 1936 to aid needy children. Funding is derived from the sale of Solstickan matchboxes. Artist Einar Nerman created the design for the matchbox based on a painting of his own son. Solstickan proceeds now support scientific research in childhood diseases.

7

THE RISE OF THE WOUNDED FEMININE IN THE MEDIA

———

The shadows are deepening all around us. Now is the time when we must begin to see our world and ourselves in a different way.
(Madeleine L'Engle.)

The rise of the wounded feminine has been my concern for a long while, even before conceiving this book: quite an overdue pregnancy!

Recently I unearthed a column I had written years ago after viewing House of Sand and Fog. I was so perturbed by this movie that I found myself writing about it in the context of the wounded feminine. So for years, even in my

165

unconscious, I have been encountering the wounded feminine in various media: books, films, plays, TV.

This chapter is by no means an exhaustive critique of our culture as it plays out in literature and the media. I hope that my mini exegesis of the few TV programs, books, and movies that I have encountered prompts us to question where the wounded feminine is rising—and isn't.

Since my own consciousness is getting raised, I find I cannot view anything without being curious as to where it fits on my Richter scale of paradigm shift: is it the rise of the wounded feminine bursting forth, or is it one more story of the feminine principle being tamped down and buried alive? I will give a few examples of both burial and resurrection.

Despite the polarities of death and resurrection at play, I am confident that the feminine principle, the wounded feminine is rising. That this tension is so visible and ubiquitous is evidence that an alchemical transformation is occurring! But let's begin with the burials.

THE BURIAL GROUNDS OF THE WOUNDED FEMININE

HOUSE OF SAND AND FOG

In 2009 or so, I viewed *House of Sand and Fog*. Fortunately, we saw it at home and not in a movie theater. My vocal responses to the actions on the screen were frequent and frequently loud.

The following is a commentary I wrote in the aftermath, but its relevance regarding the wounded feminine remains .... Having viewed *House of Sand and Fog*, I don't know if I am more disturbed by the movie or by the critics' lack of recognition of what it might be construed to portray psychologically. Hence I think that an important view of this movie is lost. It is hard to disagree with the critics when they point out the film's many technical flaws; yet, it also hard to not recall the mesmerizing grip the film placed on me and the vividness with which I recall it afterwards. On the surface, the movie is about ownership of a house—the American dream of the immigrant gone awry. Underneath the tug of war regarding home ownership between an Iranian immigrant, a colonel in the fallen Shah's Air Force, and a ne'er-do-well recovering addict who inherited the house when her father died but who has neglected to attend to tax collection notices (albeit, erroneously billed, she lacks the responsibility to open her mail to right the matter).

This film, perceived in other terms, might be instead a tragic story of what happens in a faltering patriarchy that does not heed the wounded feminine.[1]

But blood is assiduously avoided in the Behrani family—the feminine is feared.

Early on, we see the colonel admonishing his son as he arrives home from athletic practice with a wounded leg—"do not get blood on the floor"—we then see the bloody leg and immediately the scene shifts to the moon, the feminine menses symbol. One may ponder if the colonel's concern with bloody messes has a history—did

---

1. Blood in this film might be considered to be a symbol of the feminine—blood is messy, blood is the mysterious menses, the sacred mysteries of women; and blood might also be a symbol of sacrifice.

blood shedding occur at his hand under the patriarchal power of the Shah? Later, Nadi and Esmail wrap Kathy's bloody foot in a plastic bag before she crosses the threshold into their/her house and they tend to her injury.

Early in the film we see the young woman Kathy in bed waking up to her mother's phone call. She responds to her mother's inquiry about her husband with denial. She avoids the truth and tells her mother he is away on business—again. In fact, he has left her. She, we discover, inherited her father's house, a find of a beachfront property that is deteriorating in disarray under her "care." It would seem that she needs to learn how to psychically leave her father's house and move into her own adulthood. Takeout leftovers, strewn about among other garbage, and unopened mail cluttering the floor by her door indicate that she is still in a hole of despair even if she is not actively abusing drugs or alcohol. She is surrounded by the beauty of nature yet in being so disconnected from it she gains no access to its nurture for her soul.

Note that her own attractiveness seems to enamor some male film critics to the point where they can't seem to judge her actions impartially. In their critiques, they appear to collude with her. The fact that male critics downplay her responsibility in the tragedy that unfolds seems to me to be "reverse patriarchy" bias. As a woman, I do not find her an endearing character; the Iranian mother Nadi shows her more compassion than I can muster. Kathy has solid choices to make all along the way that would help her out of her hole, but time and again she digs deeper.

When I say this, however, I question how I can confer blame on her for the patriarchy in which she is trapped (my own complex activated, perhaps). Who knows what her family and father issues were before he died? And "patriarchy" is not about men per se. The patriarchal way of life wounds both men and women when it juxtaposes male dominance and authority over women, when it seeks power through might rather than collaboration, when it condones violence and eschews compassion.

The women in this movie—save the legal defense attorney—all seem caught in a patriarchal complex. Kathy, the dry drunk, cannot metaphorically leave her father's house and grow into her own identity as an adult; and so she is literally evicted. Had she done the psychological work of leaving her father's house, the tragic circumstances would not have unfolded as they did.

Nadi, the Iranian mother, is subject to the benevolence of her despotic husband. He is caught in his own rigid character structure of how a man "should" be—particularly a man of stature and authority in his home country, Iran. It is easy to empathize with his character that seems proud yet having integrity. (I remember my father always keeping his honor and pride intact by wearing his suit jacket and bow tie even when his job didn't call for that—it was his way of standing tall—and he was short—in the face of an American culture that might still consider him an Italian immigrant even though he was born here.)

The colonel is a victim of the patriarchy too—he is so engulfed in his role as male provider that he, like Kathy, is in denial of his truth. His truth is that he works many menial jobs to support his family, that his Italian suits and his Mercedes are mere phantoms of a memory of more. The Behranis live excessively beyond their means so that his daughter can be "successfully" married and they can retain their social status and their son can look forward to going to a fine college. However, whatever small fortune they took with them when they left Iran is dwindling.

And Nadi, his wife, has power and grace, but she is subsumed under his benevolent dictatorship. Theirs is a loving relationship but it is not an equal partnership. In his patriarchal world, the colonel is sometimes seen to resort to physical violence (infrequent violence accompanied with apologies afterwards remains violence). We see early in the film in flashbacks to Iran that the colonel has toppled large luscious pine trees in order to survey the ocean view "to infinity." As he orders this, we see his wife on the beach running with the children. The seeds of destruction are already sown. (At first I thought her running was in distress for what he had done with the trees but reviewing the scene, she is instead colluding with his action—women are not innocent in patriarchy either. The patriarchy, to expand the metaphor, is the energy behind destruction of, e.g., rain forests—brute force to overcome "obstacles" and whatever is "in the way" of "progress," power, money.) Nadi is caught in a gilded cage and doesn't question his authority which provides a comfortable life for her and her son. (In his succeeding to marry his daughter off to a wealthy Irani family, there became another gilded cage in the making.) Nadi pushes and pressures her colonel, playing into the patriarchy.

The deputy sheriff Burdon who attempts to "rescue" Kathy, another patriarchal gesture of "I know better even when I do things illicitly," seems to be the most unconscious complex driven figure of them all. Unhappy in his marriage, he "befriends" Kathy after he serves her the eviction notice. He drinks wine in her presence and she, of course, doesn't resist the temptation. These are two people driven by their own dark psychological complexities and neediness and they feed each other with their dysfunction. Burdon, like Colonel Behrani, uses brute force against his wife when she confronts him about his affair with Kathy.

Patriarchal power is in charge; and what the archetypal feminine symbolizes, compassion and connection, is demeaned. Both women and men need this feminine aspect to soften patriarchy's harshness.

Esmail, the son of the Behranis, would seem to be the hope for the integration of the masculine and feminine—who might carry the loving compassion and connection that tempers patriarchy's rigidity and relentless need for control. Unfortunately, he meets a tragic end, as does his father.

Instead, it becomes Kathy's choice. Unable to psychically leave her father's house, she perhaps is finally awakening to the world she must create for herself, post eviction and in the aftermath of tragedy, and with no illusions about either being sacrificed/victimized to the government's blind-to-human-plight bureaucratic patriarchy or "rescued" by the blundering power of the father authority figure of deputy sheriff Burdon. Would that she could have learned sooner that leaving her father's house was what she had to accomplish all along. There may have been less suffering. *House of Sand and Fog* drives home (pardon the pun) how inter-connected we are in our psychic woundedness. The more we heal ourselves, the more we heal the world.

THE NEWSROOM

In 2012, we have the HBO series, *The Newsroom*, which is set in the recent past and tracks real-life stories. But it is the back story of the newsroom itself that I find disturbing.

"Don't be a pussy," says Sam Watterson playing the publisher in the newsroom. Really? This demeaning phrase about women is the tip of the patriarchal iceberg into which this show has collided. How disappointed I am in the rendition of women and the feminine principle in the series by Alan Sorkin that purports to depict telling truth to power, and whose anchorman has become an Ed Murrow wannabee after being an overpaid yes-man to his network's corporate sponsors.

Yet for all the stories covered that relate to recent events, the *status quo* of the patriarchy will never be upended if women on the show are to be portrayed as emotional ditherers and second-class citizens. Mackenzie McHale, played by Emily Mortimer, the producer of the newscasts, is described as a former war correspondent who has been in harm's way, even having taken a bullet. And yet in the newsroom she continues to defer to the patriarchal anchorman whom she formerly dated. Her gutsiness is forever blunted by her unending search for approval from the men around her.

Even strong women in this program somehow seem to collapse to any masculine presence. Men rule here. Yeah, sure, Jane Fonda plays the wealthy maven CEO of this media empire. But she is hardly seen here as the feminine principled woman. Instead, she is a member of the patriarchal boys club, brimming with negative animus.

If this newsroom really intends to speak truth to power it needs to honor both the feminine principle and the women—and men—who embody it.

BOSS

Another TV series is far less ambivalent in its portrayal of patriarchy. In *Boss*, Kelsey Grammer plays the mayor of Chicago, Tom Kane, who has been diagnosed with Lewy Body disease—an illness that can only lead to debilitating dementia and death. More power-hungry and brutal than Macbeth, the mayor is a ruthless man who may have lost his soul long before he started to lose his mind. His disease has only concretized his lack of conscience in the pursuit of power. In this series, we see women of patriarchy collude with their men of power in the same immoral games. Kane's wife is a match for her husband's cunning.

Their daughter, Emma (played by Hannah Ware), is the epitome of the wounded feminine. It is unclear if this wounded feminine is indeed rising. We see her recovering from substance abuse, working as a pastoral counselor and nursing assistant in an inner city health clinic. Her father comes to her clandestinely looking for medication, not wanting to have a record of prescriptions for his disease. He seems so solicitous of her, the patriarchal father with loving heart and a caring connection with his daughter. She manages to get his drugs through illicit means and she also stocks her clinic in the same manner.

In a stroke of expediency to deflect negative press about a toxic waste dump site he allowed, and which has caused horrific cancers in children who resided in its vicinity, Mayor Kane informs drug enforcement of Emma's clinic. He sells his own daughter down the river for his political survival. We see him crying to the camera about how brokenhearted he is that his daughter has succumbed to such an illicit life.

There do not seem to be any redemptive bones left in this patriarch. Kane may not bury the wounded feminine as did Zala do to Lisbeth Salander in the Larsson trilogy, but he does imprison her.

Compared to Kane, Tony Soprano and his wife look saintly. In the *Sopranos*, Tony's daughter Meadow was the young woman who carried the feminine principle. It was she who seems to hold hope for the rise of the wounded feminine while her father was the mafia man. Her mother colluded with her father by being in denial. Yet, unlike Kane, Tony Soprano, with his panic attacks and anxiety, seems to have intermittent bouts of conscience. The mayor does not, nor does his wife, who is more callused than Lady Macbeth. Machiavellian reincarnations, these.

What does this tell us about our *zeitgeist*? Is there consciousness to the stories? Are they morality plays which give us fair warning of what road not to take? In that sense then, their burial of the feminine principle is a graphic lesson about corrupt patriarchal power. After all, the *Boss* theme song is "Satan, your kingdom must come down!"

In addition to the mayor's daughter, there is another woman of note in *Boss*. She appears to carry the feminine principle along with a strong positive *animus*. That is Mona Fredericks (played by Sanaa Lathan), the African-American who becomes his staff aide after confronting him from the other side of the aisle. We hope that she can maintain her integrity and focus as she works with the mayor. She is portrayed as a loving wife and mother as well as a feisty politician who fights for the good of the community. However, she is the lone soul, tight-roping the balance between the masculine and feminine in the mayor's dangerous universe.

This series did not get renewed. If it had been, I am curious whether the boss would rediscover his soul, and whether Emma could stand again in her own authority. At the last episode we see, Mona maintains her integrity, balancing the equation of good versus evil, by having to leave the city and start a new life. The feminine principle to be protected, rose up and went elsewhere!

COMMANDER IN CHIEF

It is always interesting to note how the feminine principle rises in certain TV programs and then gets eclipsed by bread and circus extravaganzas.

Commander in Chief started its broadcast in the fall of

2005. This show about the first female president of the United States garnered the highest ratings until the shows, *American Idol* and *Criminal Minds*, came along. (Wikipedia)

When a sitting president suddenly dies, McKenzie Allen (portrayed by Geena Davis), the vice president, becomes Commander-in-Chief. I think that this series depicted quite realistically how the country would react to a woman president. We have already experienced our nation's reaction—or should I say reactivity—to having elected Barack Obama. There have been numerous factions that resent his presidency just because he is African American. Likewise, I conjure that there would be reaction to a woman president as well.

However, what was refreshing about *Commander in Chief* was the attention to the positive aspects of her being a woman president. She carried the positive animus well, being strong and decisive, yet was also caring and compassionate. She portrayed the balance of the masculine and the feminine. I recall one episode where she went beyond pardoning the proverbial Thanksgiving turkey and pardoned an unjustly incarcerated human being! Would that that tradition be instituted in the White House.

She also invited her archrival, speaker of the house Nathan Templeton (played by Donald Sutherland), to dinner.

I remember watching these episodes delighted to see a woman leader was a commanding and caring presence. What a pity that this paradigm shift of consciousness to behold a woman president who balances the masculine and feminine so well was not yet ready for prime time: bread and circuses of escapism and violence continue to rule.

Created by David Kelly, *Harry's Law* was the TV series which had a brief run from January 2011 to May 2012. Kathy Bates portrays Harriet Korn, an aging attorney fired from a prestigious Houston law firm. She then forms her own idiosyncratic practice in the back of a Cincinnati shoe store. Like *Commander in Chief*, she is feisty and bright and carries the balance of the masculine and the feminine. We see her defending the disenfranchised and forgotten with a sardonic wit and caring wisdom.

Also, the show's themes often honed in on current and relevant issues. A range of topics included: a defense of undocumented immigrants, defense of a man already deemed guilty by the media, defense of a teen tried for murder after cyber-bullying a classmate—the girl was blamed for the death of a classmate because of her internet remarks. Highlighting the danger of traumatic brain injuries in high school football, Harry also argues on behalf of parents whose son had died as a result of a head injury in a game.

While Harry confronted issues from domestic violence to cruelty to animals, she may have sometimes gone against the grain of popular opinion both in the show and to some viewers. What I found refreshing was how *Harry's Law* was in defense of the every man and every woman. She was an articulate voice facing the powers that be.

Unfortunately, the demographics that count—younger

adult viewers—weren't watching. More bread and circus moments please—sex and violence, anyone?

This series made its debut in 2009 and continues to air, due less to its positive portrayal of women than to on-screen sexuality and political intrigue. Whatever works to keep the show going and gives center stage to women who will hold their own in the patriarchal world—without becoming daughters of the patriarchy themselves!

Juliana Margulies plays Alicia Florrick, a politician's wife and stay-at-home mother who returns to practicing law after a twelve year hiatus. We are introduced to husband Peter Florrick (played by Chris Noth) as the former Cook County state's attorney, who has been sentenced to jail for corruption as well as a sex scandal. Through many convolutions we see that he was in part framed by his political enemies—the corruption charges were dropped but the sex scandals stood.

Like her counterparts in the "real" world, Alicia Florrick stands as the "good wife" next to her husband as he launches into yet another political campaign, this time for governor.

However, central to the continuing saga is how Alicia Florrick maintains her balance as mother to two teenagers and as stiletto-heeled lawyer. Yes, while men play the power field in shoes that ground them, women wear shoes that keep them dancing on their toes.

We see Alicia needing to stand tall on those heels in a

world of male power brokers. She does so, keeping her compassion and her search for justice intact.

Likewise we see her boss, Diane Lockhart (played by Christine Baranski) as a high-powered woman who supports other women as well as liberal issues. She, despite her position as senior partner, has a compassionate conscience that pulls her occasionally to disenfranchised causes. (We see her in one episode visiting a community legal aid office, only to tell them they will no longer receive funding from the firm. The result of the visit was that she took on a *pro bono* case.)

Forsaking heels, Kalinda Sharma wears "boots of justice." So says Archie Punjabi who portrays her. Archie explains that the boots help ground her in the character—and character she is! Admittedly, Kalinda is my favorite rise of the wounded feminine woman in this series. She is the firm's private investigator and her means of fact-finding may sometimes be questionable. Yet even in her enigmatic, steely behavior there lurks a heart of compassion. I am reminded of Lisbeth Salander when I see her in action. She, like Lisbeth, seems to have been wounded along the way and is now rising to right the wrongs of others.

I also wonder about her name, Kalinda. I think she carries the dark spirit of Kali well. Kali is the Hindu goddess that embodies the dark forces of destruction and mayhem in service of the divine plan. She is the feminine aspect of God that shines light on the underbelly of life, where shadow resides.

Whether we see Kalinda stand up to the dark side wearing boots of justice or Alicia walking into a den of men (one example is a political council where she is unwelcome) speaking truth to power, or Diane remembering her feminist roots, these women are carrying their animus in service of the feminine principle.

In my view, the men overall seem far less conscious and aware. Even the males who seek justice and fair play nevertheless seem caught in patriarchy's snare. Usually they seem more smitten with pursuit of power than justice. However, there are, moments of grace. Will Gardner (played by Josh Charles) is a partner in the law firm where Alicia is on staff. According to the storyline, their relationship goes back to Georgetown Law School and the sexual tension remains. The heat between them may pique viewer interest, but I find it more compelling that Will has displayed, at least on one occasion, a sense of compassion and integrity. I recall one segment where he confronts the judge who is his basketball playing buddy. The story closely resembles what in fact did occur recently in Pennsylvania. The fictional judge, as did the Pennsylvania family court judges, received kickbacks for every child incarcerated in a private for-profit detention center. These kids were being remanded to prison for absolutely no legitimate charge, yet the judge and these juvenile prisons were making money off the traumatized backs of innocent children. In the TV *doppelgänger* of the truth, Will carries the masculine along with the feminine principle to do the right thing.

When Will pursued the case of a young boy who clearly was unjustly incarcerated and discovered that his friend was the guilty judge, Will managed to serve justice in one TV segment of *The Good Wife*. Unfortunately, his quite heroic efforts were not available to the innocent children incarcerated in Pennsylvania. It took years before the corrupt county officials were arrested.

The real life story has been examined in *Kids For Cash: Two Judges, Thousands of Children, and a $2.8 Million Kickback Scheme*, written by former *Philadelphia Inquirer* reporter William Ecenbarger. In this accounting, Ecenbarger describes how Judge Mark A. Ciavarella jailed thousands of youths in the Scranton, Pennsylvania, area—more than unjustly, unconscionably! An example? One eleven-year-old was shackled (yes, *shackled*) off to PA Child Care (a for-profit, juvenile retention facility) for having called the police after his mother locked him out of the house during an argument. Ciavarella, and his co-conspirator, Judge Michael T. Conahan, received, over the years almost three million dollars from PA Child Care for keeping their for-profit facilities at maximum capacity.

The prison developer, Robert Mericle, gave the judges money in order to build the for-profit detention facilities. Robert Powell, co-owner, was also involved in the kickback scheme in order to secure a high number of inmates. When justice was served, Powell and Mericle were jailed themselves. The longest sentences are now being served by Ciavarella and Conahan.

Truth is more horrific than fiction; and its discovery is rarely swift.

TREME: AN HBO SERIES ABOUT POST-KATRINA NEW ORLEANS

Created by David Simon and Eric Overmyer, and taking its name from a New Orleans neighborhood, *Treme* aired from the spring of 2010 through 2012. It depicts life in New Orleans after Hurricane Katrina hit in 2005 with the levees subsequently giving way to create massive flooding.

The series begins three months later as residents attempt to restore their lives. *Treme* depicts men and women on an equal footing coping with their destroyed homes, livelihood, and sometimes loss of life.

Even though the patriarchy creeps in with wheeler-dealers who want to cash in on reconstruction, even though there is the old boy network of the justice system that protects its patriarchy, there remains an egality among the residents. These chefs, musicians, teachers, attorneys, fisher people, share in the communal suffering of lives having been upended in an instant. Yet we watch as they, in their resilience, slowly come to terms with loss and find some semblance of a "new normal." The music never dies—the beat goes on.

THE HUNGER GAMES TRILOGY

Between 2008 and 2010, Suzanne Collins published for young adults the trilogy comprised of *The Hunger Games*, *Catching Fire*, and *Mocking Jay*. The stories are told in the first person by sixteen-year-old Katniss Everdeen.

The North America she knows is now called Panem—bread—and the wealthy and powerful live in the capital (which may have formerly been Denver). Seventy-five years earlier, there had been a massive destructive event—possibly a war—from which was established thirteen districts with the capital at the helm. Katniss resides in the Apalachian District, Number 12. This is one of the poorest regions.

The Hunger Games title refers to the annual bread and circus (*panem et circum*) events for which a boy and a girl from each district is chosen to compete. This televised and "sponsored" show is a competition to the death of all but one survivor.

Susan Collins has remarked in various interviews that she came upon the idea for these novels while watching TV. What arose for her in her psyche was the cultural blur between "reality TV" shows, interspersed with commercials, along with footage of the Iraqi invasion. My own reaction to her books before I heard her interview (or read Wikipedia's notes regarding her comments) was that indeed she did weave together the chaotic fabric of our culture: where violence is masked by bread and circus deflections.

What do I mean by that? Consider how we are all entertained for weeks by stories about sex scandals, some celebrities divorce, marriage, or boob exposure. Or stories about "Octo-Mom"[2] or Casey Anthony[3]— aren't we throwing breadcrumbs of distraction with circus extravaganzas while Rome burns?

2. "Octo-Mom," Nadya Denise Doud-Suleman, was roundly criticized in the media for delivering octuplets into her family of six prior children, even though she was unemployed and on public assistance.

3. Casey Anthony was accused of suffocating her infant daughter. A highly publicized trial resulted in her being found not guilty.

We are no more outraged at old white men sending young men and women to be killed and maimed in war than are the people of Panem outraged that the games are about watching children die. Like the people of the hunger games, we like our bread and circus moments.

We have been at war for over 10 years, but the human cost (let alone the monetary cost which is a huge part of our national debt) of ALL who have or are suffering the effects of violence and war takes a backseat to the TV shows that numb our consciences and our collective consciousness.

When we do take note of the death and destruction of war, we attend only to our "own." We may now hear about PTSD, TBI, wounded warriors, the mortality of our soldiers. Yet we almost never note the cost of war on the populations of the countries we invade.

As I write this, sabers rattle about Iran. Israel's prime minister Netenyahu wants the US to stand with him and prepare to bomb Iran because they may someday have nuclear capability.

Meanwhile Israel and the US already have nuclear capability to send us all to smithereens beyond the likes of Panem or its District 13 of the hunger games. So, no, unfortunately Susan Collins' hyperbolic fantasy of a post-apocalyptic North America is not so far-fetched. I can dimly (I want to keep it dim) envision it: Israel and the US bomb Iran. China bombs the US. After the nuclear holocaust and fallout destroys most of us, we are left with the Koch Brothers and the Adelsons in the great land grab, taking over Denver as their capital because they commandeered the bomb shelters deep down under the mountains of Colorado.

In *The Hunger Games*, Katniss Everdeen may be our icon of the rise of the wounded feminine. She embodies the archetype of Artemis the archer, wielding her bow and arrow with deft precision in the forests of her poverty-stricken district. Peeta Mellark is the Baker's son who bestows her with bread one day when he sees her sitting in an alley, weak with starvation. Later, they are to be pitted against each other in the games. But it is Peeta's unconditional love, misunderstood as it might be by Katniss, that helps change the dynamic of killing in the games. He, I consider, embodies the feminine principle as a male.

Collins' allegory almost portrays the masculine and feminine integrating to bring forth a balance of energies through loving connection.

In the first book we see Peeta's love and Katniss's prowess joining to defy the patriarchal violent scheme of the games: apparently, never before has love for another been introduced into the plot line of The Hunger Games, where the mayhem to the death of children is televised. However, Peeta broadcasts his love for Katniss for all to witness. As Peeta sets a new tone to the games, the totalitarian regime co-opts even love, capitalizing upon it for bread and circus effect.

At first, Snow, the authoritarian patriarch leader, agrees that both Peeta and Katniss can survive. Of course, he changes the rules at the last moment. But Katniss foils Panem's power. In front of the cameras for all the districts to witness, she and Peeta hold the deadly poisonous berries she had saved. She asserts that either both he and she live or they will both ingest the berries for all to see their death on-screen. Snow must renege to save face; nevertheless, he is enraged that this power has been so diminished.

Collins with this first story, gives us the wedding of the masculine and feminine in the vanquishing of violence. However, I have some hesitation about how the saga continues in the next two books. Collins' writing gives us graphic pictures of violence throughout the trilogy. While Katniss silently notes her disdain for the society's violence, her reflection was often displaced by the action. And Katniss, unlike Native Americans of tradition, never considers her own killing of animals as anything more than necessity. There is no thought to the interconnectedness of all life. Granted she and her family are starving, so in terms of Abraham Maslow's hierarchy of needs they are the bottom rung of the scale of self-actualization. Meanwhile, Peeta holds the bread of life here and no doubt certain Christians may have a field day with this analogy to Christ.

However, I like the fact that Peeta is not killed off to be resurrected in new form. For all the trilogy's ambivalence and lacunae, Peeta does remain unwavering in his stance of unconditional love and Katniss remains connected to him despite her bewilderment.

So, in my interpretation, the trilogy does, if imperfectly, depict the rise of the wounded feminine and the carrying of the feminine principle in both the male and female.

TRUE GRIT?

When I happened to see the movie *True Grit*, I was also reading a memoir, *I Shall Not Hate: A Gaza Doctor's Journey on the Road to Peace and Human Dignity* by Izzeldin Abuelaish. Struck by the dissonance between the two stories, I wrote the following for my column in a local online paper (*Chadds Ford Live*).

We are mistaken if we think women, simply because they are women, are kinder, gentler than men.

The great psychiatrist Carl Jung said that women carry a masculine soul (*animus*) within and that men carry a feminine soul (*anima*) within. Whether the valence of these inner qualities is negative or positive depends on a number of things. But, simply put, if a woman carries her *animus* negatively, then she can be mean-spirited, vengeful, power mongering. If a man carries his *anima* negatively, he may be ineffectual and complaining. However, if a woman carries the masculine qualities of her soul positively, she is forceful and goal-directed, yet is also compassionate. When the man carries his feminine soul qualities positively, he can be receptive, nurturing, gentle, and carries this into the world with focus and clarity and determination.

With this Jungian perspective, I happened to see the movie *True Grit*, while I was also reading *I Shall Not Hate*. Both stories arise in the wake of tragedy. Mattie Ross, the late 1800's heroine of *True Grit*, has lost her father and she is determined to avenge his murder. Dr. Abuelaish, contemporary Palestinian physician, has lost three daughters and a niece in the 2009 Israeli bombing of his Gaza home. Yet he seeks peace.

An early scene in *True Grit* attests the quick avenging of post Civil War America: Three men are publicly hanged before throngs of people—men and women—lusting for the kill. Our young teenage heroine appears unflappable to the event—perhaps considering it a harbinger of the justice she seeks for her father's murderer.

Yes, she was bright, articulate, and focused in her quest. True grit? Yes. However, when we see Mattie many years later, she appears to remain one-dimensional, with no growth of character beyond an un-developed black-white morality of vengeance: no gentle grace to temper the grit.

How vastly different the living hero, Izzeldin Abuelaish, is from the fictional heroine. In his memoir, he describes his childhood in a refugee camp in the Gaza Strip. Surely, it was a far more primitive life than Mattie's in the last century. For Abuelaish, there was no electricity, no running water, no privacy. There was, however, dirt and hunger. Says Abuelaish, "in an over-crowded refugee camp, people cling to hope by a thread that threatens to break at any moment." (page 39)

As a twelve-year-old, Abuelaish witnessed the horror of the Six Day War: pandemonium prevailed, fleeing families were separated—children and parents lost from each other. At one point, Abuelaish was sure that the Israeli soldiers rounding up everyone were going to kill them *en masse*. He survived the Six Day War only to be confronted with Ariel Sharon's bulldozing of many Palestinian family's humble homes. With the relentless and ruthless havoc that threatened families' survival, Abuelaish "learned the bitter lesson of what it means to be helpless in the face of one man's power." Nevertheless, Abuelaish managed to eventually attain a medical degree. While continuing to live in Gaza and raise a family there, he worked in an Israeli hospital as an infertility specialist.

In 2009, a year after the death of his wife from leukemia, there was another Israeli incursion into Gaza. It was in this bombing of Gaza homes that three daughters and a niece were killed. Even in the midst of the bombing, Abuelaish was straddling worlds. He called an Israeli friend, a newscaster who was broadcasting live at the time of the call. Abuelaish wailed the deaths of his family and beseeched his friend to help the wounded survivors. He pleaded over Israeli TV to get ambulances to the border so that they could get them to hospitals. Although this did occur, Abuelaish still incurred the wrath of other Israelis who blamed him for the shelling, accusing him of harboring militants, hiding guns. He says, "It was so painful to hear the truth falsified. ... I wanted the Israeli army to tell me why my home, which had harbored no militants, which was filled with children whose only weapons were love, hopes, and dreams, were fired upon." Despite the fact that Abuelaish never received any apologies or definitive answers from the Israeli government, he refuses to hate.

"My three precious daughters and my niece are dead. Revenge, a disorder that is endemic in the Middle East, won't get them back for me. It is important to feel anger in the wake of events like this; anger that signals that you do not accept what has happened, that spurs you to make a difference. But you have to choose not to spiral into hate. All the desire for revenge and hatred does is drive away wisdom, increase sorrow, and prolong strife."

Abuelaish is far more our role model than is Mattie Ross for the integration of the masculine and feminine. Jung would say that he carries the feminine *anima* soul qualities of gentleness, compassion, receptivity, and relationship as a man far better than does Mattie, the moral avenger. *True Grit* lacks the true grace of a life beyond hate.

WINTER'S BONE

David Woodrell's book *Winter's Bone* became a movie by the same name. Ree Dolly,[4] the female protagonist, is a more complex and compassionate figure than Mattie (of *True Grit*).

A sixteen-year-old girl of the Ozarks woods, she leads a hardscrabble life taking care of her younger sibs ever since her mother's mind decayed along with her beauty. Ree's father has skipped bail, having been arrested for running a crystal meth lab, sort of his family clan's business. If her father doesn't show up at the next court date, the family will lose their house. So it is that Ree sets out to find him, no matter if he is dead or alive. The kin don't take kindly to

---

4. Jennifer Lawrence portrayed Ree Dolly in the film version of *Winter's Bone* and portrayed Katniss in *The Hunger Games*. She, like Noomi Rapace who played Lisbeth in the Larsson Trilogy, seems to understand the endurance, determination and strength of her character.

Ree's sleuthing and she literally faces their brutality. They corner her in a barn, knocking her teeth out. The women of the clan, who participated in the beating, later decide to help her find her father. Evidently, they know who killed him and where his body was hidden. Under cover of night they escort her, hooded, to the place where her father's body had been left to rot. In this story, Ree is not looking so much to avenge her father's murder as much as she wants to save the family hearth. The clan can keep its secrets. She is protecting the new life that will be hers and her brothers.

In the embodiment of the interpretation of the masculine and the feminine, she does not collapse in the face of the extended family's violence. Instead, it is her courageous heart that keeps her immediate family safe and intact. How appropriate, since courage and care have the same root: *coeur*, heart. And it is also interesting that the word root itself has the same origins as radical—*radix*! The radical act of integration of "true grit"—tough courage—and "tender" care.

THE HELP

Is this the new millennium version of *Gone with the Wind*? I was most distressed in reading Kathryn Stockett's book, *The Help*. Scatological pie served to revenge the white women's racist ways or no, *The Help* smacked, to me, of a white woman riding on a white horse to rescue the African American maids who served her.

What did the rescuing of this book was the superlative performance in the movie of the various maids, particularly

Viola Davis as Aibileen Clark and Octavia Spencer as Minny Jackson. These actors, talented as they are, also seemed to channel their mothers and their grandmothers experiences with deep heartfelt sense. Hence, the movie had more emotional depth than the wimpy whiteness of the book. Nevertheless, the troubling undercurrent remained.

Tulane University professor, Melissa Harris-Perry noted how "African American domestic workers became props [for the white protagonist]." Perry articulates how *The Help* trivialized the brutality and reduced the narrative to "light Hollywood fare." Reminding us that black women were raped by their employers, Perry further notes that the South was the place of lynchings of African Americans and burnings of whole communities. To Perry, *The Help* was both troubling and in no way historical—except that it continues the myth that the fidelity of black women domestics is more important than the realities of their lives."

In spite of this, the strength and courage of the African American women in *The Help* does point to the rise of wounded feminine. No matter, pardon the pun, the whitewashing of their travails Aibileen and company do not collapse under the weight of the oppression they truly endure.

THE COLOR PURPLE

In 1982, Alice Walker published *The Color Purple* which was made into a film directed by Steven Spielberg in 1988.

Celie Harris is the protagonist and narrator. The setting is the South, early 1900's into the 1940's. Poor and uneducated, Celie is beaten and raped by her father, Alphonso, and gives birth to two children, first a girl and then a boy. Her father abducts both children, and she presumes, them to be dead. Not until later in life does Celie discover that Alphonso was not her biological father but her stepfather. Her true father had been lynched years before because he had become "too successful" as a black store owner.

Through many turns and traumas, Celie and other women in the story symbolize the rise of the wounded feminine. Alice Walker chose the title, *The Color Purple*, to be symbolic of the beauty that surrounds us. However, early on, Celie connects the color purple with pain and suffering. (See Wikipedia synopsis regarding the movie.) It is the color of the vagina that has been sexually abused. In a turn of events, it is Celie's husband's ("Mister's") paramour, Shug Avery, who opens Celie to a new way of looking at the world. In a field of purple flowers, Celie, with Shug's help, lets in the beauty of the earth.

Shug also enables Celie to expand her spirituality. For many years, Celie writes letters to God, but they are to a white male god that is disconnected and distant from her. With Shug's urgings, she begins to imagine God as genderless, colorless—an "It" that loves creation and wants human participation in that love. As Celie's spirituality deepens and matures, her independence as a woman also takes root. Symbolically, as she becomes empowered with her own inner animus, Celie starts her own business selling pants. Pants—the transformative symbol that would allow women to be equal to men. (Some material sourced from Wikipedia.)

On a September 28, 2012, *Democracy Now* broadcast, Amy Goodman interviewed Alice Walker on the thirtieth anniversary of the publication of *The Color Purple*. It is here that Walker describes the story of Celie:

It [...] is the struggle of someone who thinks she has no voice and has no place and writes letters to God because she has nobody else to write to. And then she discovers that the god that she's writing to is deaf, because he's basically the Christian god that has been imposed on black people. And at that point, she starts writing to her sister. And eventually she understands that divinity is all around us and that we are a part of it and it's in nature.

Walker also talked with Goodman about what specific scenes in the book and movie meant, for example, when Celie stands up to her husband after years of denigration. Symbolically, Celie calls her husband "Mister." Walker says that in this scene of asserting herself, Celie "curses Mister and all the misters in the world and says to them, 'Until you do right by me,' meaning herself as a person but also 'me' as the earth, 'everything you do will crumble, and everything you do will fail.'"

Walker considers Celie's words to be prophetic, and Celie understands the profundity of her message:

It comes very strongly through her [Celie] that this is true, that unless people are doing right by the poor of the world, by the downtrodden, and by women, generally, they are doomed.

Our culture, our society, our world is doomed. ... The oppression of women is global. It's not just ... in the black community. ... now people understand that this oppression of women and the abuse of children, you know, all of these things are global issues.

Yet hope lies in the very title, *The Color Purple*. Perhaps the character Shug Avery represents the divine feminine within us all. As was noted earlier, it is she who introduces Celie to love and nature. Shug tells Celie, "everything want to be loved. Us sing and dance and holler, just trying to be loved."

Walker elaborates about this to Goodman:

... She's [Shug's] explaining to Celie that ... the beauty of nature is what reminds us of what is divine, I mean, that we're already in heaven, really.

WHALE RIDER

Remember the wonderful film *Whale Rider*, seen in theaters in 2002? I think it is the story of the patriarch coming to his moment of truth when he recognizes the rise of the wounded feminine in his own granddaughter.

Based on the novel of the same name by Witi Ihimaera, the drama unfolds (as does the novel) on Whangara on the east coast of New Zealand's North Island. (The details in the book differ slightly from those of the movie.)

The central figure is Kahu Paikea Apirana ("Pai"), a twelve-year-old Maori girl whose mother and twin brother died in childbirth. She then becomes the only living child in the line of succession as tribal chief. Angry that he is left with a "worthless" girl, her chieftain grandfather, Koro, is ambivalent towards her. While he takes her to school every day on his bike, he castigates her and blames her for ongoing tribal tensions. Pai's father gets tired of his father's deprecation of him as well and decides to leave for Germany to pursue his art career and plans to take Pai with him.

However, in the midst of their leave-taking, Pai decides she cannot abandon her sea and its whales. She returns to the village and secretly takes on the warrior training her grandfather is teaching the boys. Even though Koro insists this is for males only, she desires to be chief of the tribe. It is she who learns the Maori tribal ways best, and it is she, who, unbeknownst to her bitter grandfather, dives deep into the sea to retrieve the "rei puta," whale tooth, he has cast there to be found by the true warrior chief. In his continual blindness to his granddaughter's talents in the traditional ways, he believes the whale tooth is lost forever. While Pai is at a school event where she is performing traditional chants, and telling stories that should make her grandfather proud, Koro, meanwhile, is on the beach. Earlier he had cried out to his ancient whales in despair, now a pod of them lay there, needing to be led back to the sea. He is bereft thinking this is all the fault of there being no heir to the chieftain. When Pai comes to see the whales in this lamentable state, Koro again derides her and tells her to not make things any worse by touching them. As he walks away, Pai climbs on the largest and leads the pod back to the ocean. However, Pai almost drowns in their rescue. Yet the wounded feminine does rise, Pai does regain consciousness, and her grandfather, unconscious for so long in his patriarchal trance, comes to consciousness also. He recognizes Pai as the feminine chief. She, the female whale rider, has transformed the patriarch.

What a beautiful story of not only the rise of the wounded feminine but also of the transformation of the masculine. The patriarch is not slain, but transformed, his own feminine principle within finally seen and heard as he recognizes his granddaughter for having a power equal to his.

8

A PROCESSIVE CONCLUSION

godspeak: kingdom come

you, with your point-blank fury,
what if I told you
this is all there ever was:
this earth, this garden, this woman,
this one precious, perishable kingdom.
(Lucille Clifton)

It's difficult to "conclude" when the rise of the wounded feminine and its attendant backlash is astoundingly evident every moment of every day.

I had not intended to include the following diary note, believing that since the spring of 2012, the issue of contraception and health insurance had been resolved for the benefit of all women. I print it here because as of this writing the contention remains.

May 6, 2012

I have just returned from a trip to Vietnam and Cambodia with a stopover in Singapore. There was no opportunity to visit the museum of Vietnamese women so I did not receive my formal information about the role of women and the place of the feminine principle in these countries.

However I can attest to the warmth and kindness of the people there and how much I felt as a woman treated with respect and always felt safe. There remains an underlying Buddhist ethic that seems to carry people through their traumatic history to a place of forgiving not forgetting. This sense of compassion and wisdom symbolized by both Quan Yin and the Blessed Mother was evidenced in both the representations of these models of compassion in statuary and temples and churches as well as in the behaviors and actions of the people. So perhaps the rise of the wounded feminine has been and will continue to occur there (and yet there are burials as well).

Meanwhile while I was away, the Catholic Church hierarchy deigned to chastise nuns, that is, women religious, for their non-compliance with patriarchal priorities. In other words, the religious orders of nuns have been focused on social justice issues, poverty and health care while the bishops continue to hammer away at abortion and now contraception.

Clearly the hierarchy is deflecting, certainly not genuflecting, with systemic sexual abuse and worse, rampant cover-ups and denials in their ranks: the clergy has taken up a bait and switch routine. Abortion and contraception are bogus mobilizations to obfuscate their dilemma. Instead of taking the heat about their own moral failings, they have scapegoated the feminine. When all else fails, blame the woman. Old as Eve, no?

So the hierarchy runs up against Barack Obama's healthcare contract that would mandate that health insurance at religiously affiliated hospitals include contraception. Why the uproar by the bishops when in fact this was already in place at many Catholic hospitals, and twenty-six states had already mandated such coverage? Because the patriarchs in power are feeling the sting of their own sins, and displace blame on the president and his actions—such self-righteous indignation about the separation of church and state when, in fact, such regulation would create more separation of church and state, not less. That is because this enactment would mean that women would have choice and could follow their own consciences not to mention take better care of their health.

In general, Catholic parishioners never get scolded for using contraception. It would be the rare pastor indeed who would breathe fire and brimstone about birth control. Why? Because most of the parishioners with their "two kids" families have always used contraception and any hint that they could not would quickly affect the bottom line of the donation basket.

Abortion? Sure they wax on about abortion, because if parishioners are free to use contraception, chances are it is usually a non-issue. It is about those "others" who are less fortunate, or more "loose." Those unwed mothers who are faceless, nameless nobodies who know no better. They are fair game from the pulpit.

One does not have to be an activist advocate of abortion to know that to have it be safe, legal and rare is far better than the unsafe alternatives. The energy focused on ending abortion could be better used to prevent pregnancy in the first place. Or to care for all the children who are born!

What about all the other abortions that occur in the putdown of the feminine principle? Is it not abortion to arrest the development of children once they are born by lack of nutrition and health care? Is it not abortive to destroy nature in the name of corporate greed?

There are so many ways life and the feminine principle is killed. Why is that not a horror?

Sexual abuse is abortion: it is life sucking and soul wounding.

Environmental degradation is abortion: it kills the natural world.

Corporate greed is abortion: it kills all respect for the rights and needs of human beings in its thirst for money and power.

Violence is abortion: guns abound and children are killed.

So why is it that the church and the ultra-conservatives are so focused on women and reproduction? Could it be that it is the feminine principle and its power that they fear? Could it be that if the feminine principle and women were not so shackled there would be a true end of patriarchy as we know it? From the Catholic Church to the tea party to the Taliban, there is a fear of the feminine—not just women, but the feminine principle.

And so along with women, abortion and contraception why not nail the nuns? These are the women who have been the bulwark of faith. They have been the ones teaching, nursing, tending people hands on. (Not sipping whiskey and smoking cigars after every confirmation like the patriarchal bishops are known to do.)

Recently, sad to say, a woman, not a nun, but a Harvard

law professor, Mary Ann Glendon, published her commentary, "Still Hoping for Change on Religious Freedom" in the *Washington Post* (April 7, 2013). Here, she asserts that the federal regulation mandating that all employers fund insurance coverage for "sterilization, contraception, and drugs that can cause abortions" is a threat to religious liberty.

And how is the religious liberty and conscience of the employee to be maintained without this mandate? To my mind, I have a conclusion quite the opposite of Glendon's. This law bolsters separation of church and state in that it allows the individual, the employee, to decide how to utilize health insurance benefits and not be dictated to by the employer.

Glendon writes that we should be concerned about religious freedom. I am concerned: religious freedom implies I can follow my conscience and my health provider's advice without interference from my employer, no matter who they are.

I am also concerned that a woman of Glendon's stature would not see the wisdom of this mandate, and applaud it for the sake of women and families across America. Glendon aligns herself with the Catholic hierarchy; Sr. Joan Chittester lives the gospel.

RADICAL FEMINISM OR LIVING THE GOSPEL?

The Leadership Conference of Women Religious (LCWR) continues to be under the scrutiny of the hierarchy of the Catholic Church, because they say the work of the nuns has been "tainted by radical feminism." Sr. Joan Chittister, O.S.B., a Benedictine nun, author, and speaker notes (p. 30):

After thousands of years of life-giving service to the church at poverty level—building its schools, its orphanages, its hospitals, its missionary outposts, its soup kitchens, its homes for the indigent, its catechetical centers—the nuns are told the problem with their work is that it has been "tainted by radical feminism?" And by a group of men whose chance of knowing what the term "radical feminism" even means is obviously close to zero?

Chittister chides the hierarchy for describing nuns' work as in any way "tainted." Indeed, she reminds them and us, "Working to elevate the role and status of women around the world ... is at the center of the gospel."

Jesus is the sister's model for attending to women. In His time on earth, women were, at best, second class. Chittister relates (p. 30):

He [Jesus] brought back to life a little girl who by very reason of her femaleness was considered worthless in that society—and in many societies now, and in all of them to some extent. How better to demonstrate the real value of a woman than to raise her to life again? ... The church now has as its model, it seems, a man who is committed to the poor. ... It is impossible to say you ae committed to the poor and not know that two-thirds of the hungry of the world are women who get only the leftovers after their husband and children have eaten; two-thirds of the illiterate of the world are women enslaved by their lack of education as the chattel of men; two-thirds of the poorest of the poor, according to U.N. statistics, are women. It is simply impossible to be really committed to the poor and not devote yourself to doing something to change the role and status of women in the world.

As the developing Shriver Report on women, to be released in January, 2014, demonstrates with sobering clarity, to invest in women is to strengthen their husbands and children, their families and nations, their economic level and social status, their institutions and their intellectual contributions to the world at large.

From where I stand, if that's what it is to be "tainted by radical feminism," then finally, finally, let the Gospel begin in this entire church.

What if the new Pope Francis makes Sister Joan a cardinal to become a feminine voice behind the papal throne?

CARE IN THE WORKPLACE

Choice in health insurance is just one aspect of care in the workplace. Concern and respect for the employee is as important as a living wage. When the workplace regresses to Dickensian, there is no feminine principle to be found.

I hear stories where the scripts could so easily be re-written—no need for a magic wand. Recently, I heard a story about a nursing assistant who works hard at her job taking care of other people's needs. One day, her father dies in a tragic accident, and her world falls apart—as it is wont to do in traumatic grief. She has difficulty returning to work and then she has her own mishap with a bad fall—another thing that occurs when we are pre-occupied and under stress. We are prone to injuries and accidents. I know this one first hand!

So what does her employer do? Fire her. This woman, who always worked hard, has her life unravel even more. Just when she needs health insurance for her injury, she loses it. You can, with minimal imagination, figure out what happens next. If you're living paycheck to paycheck, the next thing you know you either can't pay the mortgage or the rent.

What if the story were different? What would happen if employers, especially in the health care field who should know better, would show understanding and empathy? What if they had said to this dedicated caregiver, "it looks like your grief is overwhelming you, how about we help you find counseling," or "how about a leave of absence while we keep your health insurance going?" "How can we help you, who have helped so many for so many years?" Instead the workplace often regresses into a Charles Dickens universe of un-redemptive and reactionary Scrooges.

What if the workplace Scrooges could meet their Christmas ghosts in the present moment rather than out of the past? Script change now instead of repentance at the end of the story? Surely, that would be a lot more helpful to individuals such as this nursing assistant.

So what if I did have a magic wand? I'd wipe away the bottom line mentality of the workplace and replace it with respect and care for the employees.

There are some companies that understand that such positive regard for their employees creates a good environment not only for the worker, but also for the clients and customers they serve. Would that more workplaces take Charles Dickens to heart.

I related this story of the nursing assistant at a talk I was giving on the Rise of the Wounded Feminine in the Larsson trilogy.

After the presentation, a female psychologist approached me with her own story of an uncaring workplace where she had been mistreated. The very places where we expect the feminine principles of partnership, compassion and care to be upheld we often find the dark side at play instead. This is not gender specific. Women employers or supervisors can be card-carrying members of the patriarchy as well as any man *sans* feminine principle.

In fact a client recently related to me yet another personal story from her workplace. The women owners of the "health and wellness" company where she is employed often appear to be less than feminine principled, more patriarchal bottom line without considering the employees' "health and wellness." However, my client's latest story went beyond the pale. Coming up on the schedule was to be a fourteen-hour Saturday stint. One of the employees who was assigned this event wanted to be excused due to a sudden death of a close friend of her family. Of course, she wanted to attend the funeral. Her employer said, "No. you can't go unless you get someone to replace you." My client, ever the giver, usually jumps in to save the day. This time, however, she had already made other plans and after a few years of therapy has learned to say, "No" to her employer. There may be other employees who could have pitched in, but the real bottom line is that the employer herself could have worked for just a few hours so that the young woman could attend the funeral. How heartless and un-feminine principled these employers were in this case. Once again patriarchal attitudes go beyond gender.

Ironically on the same day I heard this story, I heard another workplace saga, this time from a man. When he worked at a well-known amusement and entertainment park, a place he loved in many ways, he began to see the under belly of his dream job. One day at a meeting where "cast members" come together to celebrate some positive action among them, he has his epiphany. At this place of employment, everyone receives costumes to wear. However, the employees must buy their own shoes to the regulations of the corporation. Thus, shoes can be expensive.

The convening staff, he finds, were celebrating the fact that the employees all contributed money to buy shoes for the custodian who could not afford them himself. Everyone in the room cheered; my client sat there dumbfounded, that his cast member mates would find this endearing. "Why," he thought, "should the custodian not be paid enough to buy his own shoes and why are employees taking responsibility for what the employer should be doing? Yes, of course, he understood the compassion of the other cast members. The care they showed for each other and for the visitors was what he loved about his work, but this workplace had its lurking shadow.

Of course, these American stories of patriarchal bottom line pale in comparison to what happens in sweatshops around the globe that supply the Walmarts and the Gaps that fill our land.

On April 24, 2013, one thousand textile workers died when their unsafe factory building collapsed. The patriarchal bottom line is even thicker and bolder in these sweatshops where there are no emergency exits, no bathrooms, no breaks. There are, however, long hours in sweltering and overcrowded conditions.

While these working conditions seem vastly different than the American work experiences related here, there is a major commonality. Whether so extremely egregious that employees die, or so thoughtless and heartless that employees' responsible requests are disregarded, the patriarchal bottom line is the same. And that is: money and profit is the immoral compass. Respect for and care of the employee is of no consequence. All these stories then are on the continuum of the feminine principle of care and relationship being flagrantly wounded.

The Wounds of Poverty and Hunger Are Here

Not long ago, I attended a county mental health advisory Board meeting and did not like what I heard: that there is a rising population of the homeless hidden among the affluent. A school administrator reported how he encounters children every day in his suburban school district who are in need of food and shelter.

When we hear the word "homeless" we, unfortunately, need to expand our images from the lonely man, chronically mentally ill, who has been discharged from the state hospital ten years ago.

Include now working families living out of their cars or hopping from acquaintance to friend for shower and bed. These are real cases in our community. We used to have strong safety nets but with the tea party tenor of the times those safety nets are being ripped asunder.

After the meeting as I drive back to my office I turn on NPR. Synchronistically, I hear being interviewed two documentarians, Lori Silverbush and Kristy Jacobson discuss hunger in America. They have just directed their film, *A Place At the Table*, which aired in March, 2013. They noted that 80% of the families receiving food stamps (the SNAP program) are working full-time. In other words, many hard working Americans are not earning a living wage. These researchers also report that there are children in the schools who can't concentrate for lack of nutrition. Our brains do funny things to us when we are hungry, actually starving for the nutrients we lack even if we appear "well-fed". One little girl in the film says she is told to focus but when she looks at her teacher she imagines her to be a banana... She is malnourished. Silverbush and Jacobson cite the term "food insecurity" because the hunger may be invisible hidden in the bodies of those who are obese due to lack of proper diet and nutrition. Cheap and filling food is not usually healthy food.

Meanwhile the expectation is that churches will do it all. I am a Red Cross volunteer and I know how difficult it is to recruit volunteers. Volunteerism can be inconsistent and spotty, and we are all busy! So we expect the homeless and hungry to be cared for with stop-gap emergency measures in the basement of the non-profits. Yes, these are great assets to a community but they depend on volunteers and cannot serve everyone. Moreover, the fact that we need them in the first place is scandalous!

That the need for food banks and shelters is on the rise is a disgrace in an affluent, developed country. The greatest nation in the world we are wont to say.

We may think, what, whoa, not in my neighborhood! I live in a prosperous county of Pennsylvania, yet on my drive from that mental health meeting, the story of homelessness and hunger was being played out before me. I noticed in the coffee shop I visited, a woman sleeping in the corner, big bags at her feet. I thought, hmm, this may be her safe place of refuge for a few hours. Not 15 minutes later, I noticed a man with a burlap sack on his back, other scruffy bags in hand, walking along the road. My guess is that he is holed up somewhere in the woods between the Mc-mansion housing developments. Between the wall of gilded plutocracy and the wall of leaden patriarchy, humanity is being crushed.

There is a story of Wonder Woman where she and her male cohort are trapped between two monstrous steel walls that are closing in on them. Wonder woman, of course, saves the day. But it is not the archetype of one strong goddess we need here to power away the smothering walls of patriarchy and plutocracy. What we need here is the power of the feminine principle infused in all our actions no matter what they are. The patriarchy in its rigidity is sterile callousness; the plutocracy in its greed is inflated hubris. Both can be transformed when the feminine principle of <u>relationship</u> and care and connection is invited in.

THE IMPORTANCE OF RELATIONSHIP

Environmentalist Kathleen Dean Moore passionately urges us to consider the environmental crisis as a deeply moral issue (*Sun*, December, 2012). I wonder if the morality of the crisis is lost on many people because it is about *relationship*—our relationship to earth.

Recall that Carol Gilligan's book, *In a Different Voice: Psychological theory and Women's Development*, published in 1982, was a refutation of Lawrence Kohlberg's work. In his research on the stages of moral development, Kohlberg indicated that girls generally reached a "lower" level than did the boys.

Gilligan argued that Kohlberg's measurements of moral development were based on reasoning rather than on *relationship*. The importance of care and relationship in moral decision making was disregarded. Hence the feminine principle was dismissed.

I see this dismissal on a microcosmic level as displayed

in the verticality of linear thinking versus the expansiveness and connection of non-linear horizontal way of thought.

In Acadia National Park recently, I met an old time Mainer as well as a sundry tourist or two. It was the men who talked about the frivolity of global warming. "Yeah, global warming, I shoveled six feet of snow" said the Lake Tahoe, California, visitor. One Maine resident noted how he was waiting for Florida to come North. All were comments of not seeing the big picture of how everything is interconnected and in relationship. It is an attitude of "What I do in my little world is what is important and moral," if you will.

The Down Easter I spoke to, whose family of origin harkens back to colonial times, carries with him his ancestral attitude toward government. He describes how his relatives early on left for Canada because they were British sympathizers. They returned when the War for Independence was over, not particularly fond of either the British or the new found government. Yet he waxed on about his constitutional rights being trampled on now because the park wouldn't let him do certain things—for example, go to the beach with a metal detector.

It would appear that, for him, morality had nothing to do with relationship to the environment.

Horses may need blinders so as not to stray and lose focus or not get spooked. We humans wear blinders when we think vertically with narrow focus that does not account for relationship to the earth and to others. For the feminine principle to flourish, the blinders must come off.

"April Is the Cruelest Month" (T. S. Eliot)

April 16, 2013

As I am pondering the tragic events at the Boston Marathon where three people have died and over 170 people have been injured in two bomb blasts, I look out my family room windows to sight a robin gathering dried grass to line her nest. He flies away with his cache to return later to search for more construction material among this hill of daffodils. Robins are so feminine principled: the female builds the nest while the male gathers the building supplies. What collaboration!

Later, after work, I have a few minutes before sunset to go to a garden—Winterthur to visit the "sundial area." I am enthralled with the aromas of blending bridal wreath, quince, magnolia. Bees sound a steady bass to the array of birds twittering (the originals) and flitting into the thick of the bushes and out again. What a busy-ness before evening descends. So delicious, I need this natural beauty to heal our souls from suffering.

April 18, 2013

My thoughts and feelings pendulate between suffering and the beauty of spring. At sunset, I go to attend an impromptu call to worship at Birmingham Meeting. The intention is to gather in a spirit of love and healing in quiet reflection to encounter the violence and suffering in response to the Boston Marathon bombings that occurred on April 15, 2013.

So I wend my way through the velvet hills of Meetinghouse Road (yes, all over eastern Pennsylvania there are Meetinghouse Roads that lead to Quaker places of worship built in the 1700's and

1800's.) I see a purple swath amidst these pastures. Ah, the grape hyacinths are in full bloom. I stop at the split rail fence to see these beauties close at hand—and then I grab my cell phone for its camera. I smile. Deep purple blanket here again!

I am at the bright side of my pendulation between polarities when I am in nature. I go to meeting to hopefully "hold in the Light," as Quakers are wont to say, all those who are suffering and mourning. It doesn't matter how far or how near they are—the healing touch has no bounds.

I suddenly remember that stone meetinghouse and the spring field, now purple, across the road were witness to the carnage of a revolutionary war battle. In fact, outside the wavy glass of old windows lie the buried remains of countless unnamed soldiers.

My mind pendulates again to sending loving kindness, not only to those suffering in the aftermath of an ongoing tragedy, but also to the perpetrators that they may find their own light that remains an ember of goodness in their hearts, despite the evil they have done.

What is the trauma they carry that has led them to enact such atrocities against others? I pray that they find healing in their own souls so that they turn away from darkness and return to the light within.

APRIL 19, 2013

I woke to discovering today that my daughter and her fiancé are in shelter in place (lock down) in their apartment in Cambridge, Massachusetts. One suspect in the marathon bombings has been killed and his younger brother, the other suspect, is at large. Watching television intermittently, between my scheduled clients, I am overwhelmed with feelings. My antidote is to take a few minutes from the unfolding tragic story to visit the cherry blossoms at another garden, Longwood. I take my place in the stand of grandly gnarled trees as white and pink petals float about me. Before taking leave of Longwood, I stop by the garden shop to buy some baby gifts—two young feminines, unwounded, recently born.

One of the saleswomen remarks about the situation in Boston. I respond that my daughter is sheltering in place in her apartment while her friends in Watertown have been evacuated. The conversation with these saleswomen carries an undercurrent of compassion not only for the victims of the bombings, and the residents in lockdown, but also for the young man, one of the alleged perpetrators, who is at large. We talk about how this nineteen year old could have had a wonderful future but instead chose the dark path of his elder brother. Then, the other saleswoman discloses that she avoids watching the news because she was a Pan Am flight attendant and was in London at the time of the Lockerbie bombing. Eight of her colleagues died on that flight and she herself carries the trauma. "Good for you to take care of yourself by not watching all the news. Don't re-traumatize yourself." I say.

APRIL 21, 2013

When my daughter and son were infants and toddlers, I could not bear to hear or see news about children the age of my little ones dying or being harmed. I remember in 1980, when a jet crashed into the Potomac in Washington D.C. and there was a baby on board, I was overwhelmed with sadness. Furthermore, I was traumatized; I was fearful. As my children grew, my reactions to others' traumas paralleled whatever the age they were. Not that tragic

216

stories have not always touched me whatever the age of the child or adult, but I especially resonate to those who seemed closest to my heart.

Sadly, I am reminded of this tendency when I opened the newspaper and find the photo of Sean Collier, the MIT police officer who was killed in a confrontation with the brother bomber in Boston. He and his probable killer, Tamerlan Tsarnaev, were both twenty-six years old. Collier's photo bespeaks of a kind and gentle soul who looks like my own son. I cry—I feel a deep empathic connection with this young man who reminds me of my own flesh and blood. What bitter irony that he and one of his assailants, who later dies, were twenty-six years old. Why one young man would direct his life to public service and the other to violence is a question that deserves answers.

My point here, however is about how the more we make connections with how the other, including a stranger, is like us, the more open and empathic we are. Thich Nhat Hanh reminds us again and again that we are interbeings.

We need to grow the circle of likeness and similarity to include all people, even an enemy, so that we can be connected and empathize with the world. Such inclusivity is a cardinal sign (not sin)—rather than a red flag—that the feminine principle is operative.

Assuredly, if anyone in my family were killed or injured, my first reaction would not be from any lofty heights. My limbic system would fire up and I would want vengeance and be as furious as a grizzly bear protecting her cubs. This fact is the crux of the matter. It is because I as a victim/survivor could see red that the community and culture that surrounds me need to temper my fury seeking justice and following the law.

And then there are those who do manage to climb out of their limbic system's reactive clutch and find their center of loving kindness in the midst of, or in the aftermath of, violence. Nelson Mandela and others imprisoned developed a perspective where they saw their captors in their humanness, beyond the violence.

I am reminded of a story told by Everett Worthington a psychologist who began studying forgiveness in 1990, with an emphasis on reconciliation in couples and families. While involved in his research, his mother was murdered in her home.

Most impressive was how Worthington described his early experience of his body shaking in rage and his mind reeling in revenge fantasies to eventually being able to meet his mother's murderer to hear his own traumatic story that lead him to his crime.

This is not about "bleeding heart liberalism." If we really want transformation in our world and an end to violence, then we must connect the dots between that violence and how society and the powers that be – the patriarchy if you will – beget it.

What systemic family therapists such as Murray Bowen and Norman Paul intuited years ago, that trauma and its attendant stress cascades down the generations, has now been researched and proven. For example, numerous studies have explored the generational effects of the holocaust not only on the survivors but also on the children and grandchildren of those survivors. Whenever there is trauma from any violence, and the feelings are not faced directly, but go underground, the emotional history is carried in a new dysfunctional form.

With every war, every drone strike, every soldier deployed, the powers that be, in addition to killing and maiming, engender post-traumatic stress in all involved: the "warriors," the "enemies," and never forget, the victims/survivors of "collateral damage."

Life is always more complicated than principle cause and effect, there are many variables involved that give rise to one individual advocating violence versus another striving to never inflict the violence that he or she had been subjected to. Hitler was horribly abused as a child and that certainly compounded whatever else was in his "development" that led him to be a ruthless killer. Another man similarly abused but with a set of different variables becomes a caring father eschewing violence, perhaps changing the generational dysfunction forever so that his sons, and their sons too, truly become gentle-men.

Consider how Timothy McVeigh, a veteran of the Gulf War, witnessed his buddy's having been blown apart in Desert Storm. How did his PTSD (posttraumatic stress disorder) influence his antigovernment sentiments to precipitate his bombing of the Mirrah Federal Building in Oklahoma City. Consider also, the Washington, D.C. sniper, John Allen Muhammad (formerly Williams). He too, was another Gulf War veteran.

We have met the enemy and the enemy is us. Terrorism is not just about the other, the foreign enemy. It is about the terror of wars and conflicts that big governments such as ours (but not exclusive to us) inflict upon the innocent who then become insurgents. I am wondering aloud when I say, "when Palestine and Israel are at peace, so will the world be." Three of the great religions of the world claim Palestine/Israel as being their spiritual (and also physical for Israelis and Palestinians) home. Christians, Palestinians,

*and Jews consider Jerusalem the epicenter of their sacred space.
Instead it is the epicenter of violent eruptions. Ironic that such violent turmoil over territory should have such Biblical roots and pro-
portions. There has been cruelty and violence wielded from all
sides. The trauma of the holocaust and subsequent violence has
emboldened a faction of Israelis and Jews globally to be blind to
their own oppression of the Palestinians. The oppressed has become
the oppressor. This is not the popular view that I state. So be it. The
trauma history of the Israelis encourages the traumatization of the
Palestinians. Such deep wounds.*

*We are appalled at the violence of a suicide bomber in Israel;
yet remain silent when hundreds of people die in an Israeli shelling,
or when Palestinian houses and olive groves are bulldozed to make
way for Israeli "settlements." I see the American story of the genocide of Native Americans being repeated here. The colonials came
to flee religious oppression only to oppress and usurp land from the
Native Americans, who are then called savage terrorists when they
fight back. Until we see that the violence of the powers that be is as
reprehensible as the violence committed in retaliation we remain
in patriarchy's death grasp of domination.*

SPEAKING OF NATIVE AMERICANS, WHAT ABOUT GUNS?

In a conversation with a friend about how terror(ism) begets
terror(ism), my friend tells me that her family immigrated
to south of what would later become Pittsburgh, Pennsylvania, hundreds of years ago when white "settlers" perceived
the Native Americans as terrorists. She remembers stories
passed down the generations of an Indian massacre where
two brothers hunting in the woods came back to their farm

to find no one and nothing left. Her recollection jogged my memory as well. My husband and I lived in the northern countryside of Pittsburgh and on a truly dark and stormy—ice stormy—night we got stranded on a back road just a few miles from home. The road may have been called "Sandy Hill" but that night it was paved with slick ice. We shimmied and skid our way up the slick white to a little house on a hill. The couple inside welcomed us in—I with baby bundled in my arms, our toddler carried by my husband. Their living room was packed with other neighbors unable to drive. When I say neighbors—no house was near another, this being farm country—everyone knew each other. We were strangers here. Listening that night, I discovered most of these folks hailed from families that had lived in these hills for hundreds of years. Someone, it may have been our hosts, told the story passed down the generations of Native Americans who murdered "settlers" of their geneology. We all know the end of the story. Despite the Native American "terrorists" the whites dominated the land and the Indians were obliterated. There is also evidence that the prevalence of guns related not only to "settling" the frontier but to "controlling" the slaves of the south.

"Could it be, my friend wondered, that the American "need" for guns stems partly from pushing the boundaries of the frontier and against the Native Americans." So much of the American psyche so engrained generationally over hundreds of years that to dominate and hold the land against the "other," the dark skinned Native American, there must be guns? Does white America feel so psychologically threatened that it fears its own annihilation so it annihilates others first? This is dominator, patriarchal thinking—the thrust for power and control "over" and "against" rather than collaboration or sharing "with."

Listening to NPR as I drive one night, I hear a young woman being interviewed about her reactions to the Boston Marathon bombings of April 15 (2013). "Why? Why? Why did they do this?" she cries. "Innocent people were killed for what" are her unspoken words beneath the lament.

Later in the program comes a story of drone attacks in Wessab, Yemen. The villagers there cry out the same questions as the young American. "Why? Why?" again, they plead, "Why are innocent people being killed?"

Both bombings are violent acts against people and place. Both violent acts perpetuate the literally "vicious" cycle.

Drones fly over villages in the hinterlands of far away countries and we Americans are clueless as to the mayhem and maiming they bring. Our TV screens rarely, if ever, display the death and devastation of the Iraqi and Afghan wars, and the stealthy drone attacks that continue. We do not realize that our bombings inflict some form of 9/11 trauma on others every day. In fact, the Yemeni writer and activist, Farea Al-Muslimi testified at a U.S. Senate Judiciary Committee (April 232, 2013) that a drone attack hit his village right after the marathon bombings. Al-Muslimi garnered a scholarship to study at a high school in California. Remembering his American family fondly, he returned to Yemen

222

enamored with the U.S. Since the drone strikes on his country and, now, his village, he is baffled. He worries about his friends and family safety, as well as his own. Moreover, because the drone attacks kill innocent people, as well as Al Qaeda operatives, Al-Muslimi asserts they have become recruitment tools for terrorists. To the Senate he states, "What radicals had previously failed to achieve in my village, one drone strike accomplished in an instant."

Let me be clear: I do not condone violence of the oppressed or the oppressor. I am no more enamored of, for example, the Palestinian suicide bomber than I am of Israel's weapons of mass destruction However, I can understand, while I cannot condone, where the actions of the desperate and oppressed originate.

So here is my answer to the American young woman who asked "Why?" You are embedded in the most powerful country in the world. This power, while often used to the good, also wields its own weapons of mass destruction against the innocent. Oh, the powers that be call this collateral damage. Tell the mother whose children die in a drone attack that her beloveds are merely "collateral damage." When you begin to see that the U.S. is also a perpetrator of violence and you see that others suffer relentlessly at our hands, then you may ask why in a new way: Why is violence being perpetuated and institutionalized by the land of freedom?

Given what Al-Muslimi has voiced what would I say to the villager who weeps for her children: what about her "Why?" My response: you have suffered greatly at the hands of a great nation and for that I am sorry. I want you to know that America still does, at heart, stand for justice and liberty and that Americans, in the main, are good people. However, they are ignorant of their collective sins, that is, what the powers that be enact.

I would hope that, instead of exacerbating the violence with your young men seeking revenge, that we could cry out together to avert the carnage. Would that your young men could find their voice in lieu of violence to speak truth to the powers that be, to shout for justice and peace, not vengeance.

The powers that be—the U.S., Israel, Russia, China—may not take the high road, but you can be a model to them for how justice is wrought. Rain down on them with non-violent actions and a new world of words.

WORD(S) NOT (S)WORD

There is power in the vulnerability of the oppressed because dominator power contains within its hubris shell, the seeds of its own destruction.

Martin Luther King's Letter from Birmingham prison was a "sleeper" at first. Yet his non-violent way overcame the powers that be that violence by the oppressed never could have accomplished. Non-violence should never be confused with non-action.

King's letter castigated the moderate whites of America—including Christian Church leaders—for wanting the civil rights movement to wait: don't rock the boat, don't make waves, was the message. He reminded them that

Christ did not mollify the mainstream status quo but was instead a radical shifter of consciousness.

Taking non-violent action can precipitate simmering institutional violence to come to a visibly virulent boil. Actually King was counting on evil to erupt in its ugliness. When Bull Connor unleashed attacking dogs and the brutality of fire hoses, the nation finally came to attention and President John F. Kennedy did too.

King likened himself to Christ the non-conformist who pushes against the evil within the powers that be. Earlier in this book, we saw how Lisbeth Salander was a non-conformist who also pushed against institutionalized evil. I am reminded of the Hindu Goddess Kali, who allows for destruction to occur in order for creation to be renewed. She is an archetype for the disintegration of old forms in the service of life. King's non-violence allowed for the evil of racism to unmask itself: Once named, seen, it lost its chokehold.

Salander enacted Kali's archetype too, when she did not kill her half brother but instead made a phone call to his motorcycle gang enemies, letting them know where they could find him. In no way do I want to minimize the profound reality of the civil rights movement by making comparisons to a character in a novel—yet the similarities of confronting institutionalized evil remain.

Reading John Rieder's *Gospel of Freedom* which parses King's letter from the Birmingham jail (April 12, 1963), I am humbled by how King and the civil rights leaders and activists kept on in their non-violent "fight" against blatantly institutionalized evil. They are jailed, beaten, humiliated—and some are killed. Yet they keep on. King ends his letter not with hostility and bitterness, but with hope for relationship and connection (in Rieder p. 185):

> *Let us all hope that the dark clouds of racial prejudice will soon pass away and the deep fog of misunderstanding will be lifted from our fear-drenched communities, and in some not too distant tomorrow, the radiant stars of love and brotherhood will shine over our great nation with all their scintillating beauty.*

WHAT IS SO RANDOM ABOUT VIOLENCE?

Entropy is the degree of randomness in a system. However, with this randomness, the collisions of molecules create larger entities than their invisible selves.

So is this an analogy for what seems to be random events in the world? That incidents collide into the formation of overriding meaning larger than any singular particular context?

This morning I plant clematis: these roots I bury in the ground to resurrect, I hope, into brilliant bursts of color. As my hands work the soil, my mind meanders. Stories bump into one another—the entropy of mind hardly feels like a stream (of consciousness). Nevertheless, patterns of the wounded feminine take form. The burials and the resurrections.

Where there is violence, there is the burial of the feminine principle. Yet whenever there is any "outing" of the woundedness and burials, there is resurrection. While these burials and resurrections are not only evidenced in stories of women and girls, the fact that the abusive experiences of females is being exposed for the violence that it is in itself is a resurrection of the feminine principle.

Consider Malala Yousafzai, the Pakistani twelve-year-old student who spoke out against the Taliban in 2009. After she started blogging for the BBC under a pseudonym, she was almost mortally wounded by militants. The journalist Mudassar Shah stated, "Malala knew that she was a direct target, and yet she raised her voice. That is the difference between Malala and other people, including me." (*The Progressive*, February, 2013, p. 21) The raising of her voice is the rise of the feminine principle. Even after having been shot, she speaks out against violence and aggression and especially for the children and women of Pakistan.

Before I read about Malala's activism which almost led to her martyrdom, I met Osama—not the Osama that most know—but the anonymous Osama of a movie named eponymously. Set in Afghanistan and written and directed by Siddiq Barmak, *Osama* (played by Marina Golbahari) tells the story of a young girl whose family circumstances necessitated her to disguise herself as a boy in order to work. Her father and uncle were killed during the Soviet invasion; her mother is no longer employed. Not only has the Taliban forbidden women to work, they also cut off funding for the hospital where her mother had been a nurse. Hence, grandmother and mother convince this pre-teen to become the wage earner.

A young male friend discovers the ploy and names her "Osama." She manages the masquerade until she is mandated to attend a boy's school. Her fear of being found out is palpable throughout the movie; and her terror when she reaches menarche and the clerics discover her secret is excruciating to watch. They tie her and suspend her to a wall as she wails for her mother. The sense of her abandonment and this darkness of her place reminded me of Christ's words on the cross when he cried out, "Father, why have you abandoned me?"

Only for Osama there was no resurrection. Although not executed, we see her at the end of the film being taken off by an old man to become yet another wife, literally held captive to his whims. Would that stories like this be "only a movie."

THE TOXIC MASCULINITY CONTINUUM

Jaclyn Friedman, Executive Director of Women, Action, and the Media, and editor of the anthology, *Yes Means Yes!: Visions of Female Sexual Power and a World without Rape*, uses the term, "toxic masculinity." In an interview with Amy Goodman on *Democracy Now* (May 9, 2013), she explains: "It [toxic masculinity] really expresses something that we see all over the culture, which is men trained to think that the way to be a man is to have power over and to dehumanize women."

Goodman interviewed Friedman after Cleveland kidnap victims, Amanda Berry, Gina DeJesus, and Michele Knight, escaped their captor, suspect Ariel Castro, after ten years of (alleged) physical and sexual abuse.

Friedman does not consider the charged man to be an outlier or anomaly, but instead, "an extreme example of a pervasive dynamic in our culture which is one of toxic masculinity."

Juan Gonzalez, Goodman's colleague on *Democracy Now*, questioned Friedman about the role of the police department. Apparently, neighbors had called the police several times to come to Castro's house and there was little follow-up. While it was known that Castro had severely beaten his ex-wife in 1993 and 2005, justice was never served. Friedman notes that when the media and police pay attention to the physical abuse done to wives and ex-wives, then "We'll be getting somewhere." Our cultural lack of attention to abuse is on the continuum of violence. And our considering it justified is even more deplorable. Remember the comment to me at my community fair? "Just don't gossip," said the upstanding white man in reference to the colonial woman's punishment as being just deserts in contemporary America. The continuum of violence continues.

FROM FACT TO FICTION

What occurs in real life has its parallels in fiction to all the more accentuate the convergence of a new consciousness arising from the graves of the wounded feminine.

Contemporaneous to the unfolding of the Cleveland kidnap story, PBS presented the British mini-series, *The Bletchley Circle*. During World War II, the four women protagonists of the story had been brilliant decoders of German military offense, while working in the top-secret security headquarters of Bletchley Park, London. The year 1951 finds them, however, leading anonymous lives with no one, not even their spouses, recognizing the importance of their skills in ending the war.

One of the quartet, Susan begins to see a pattern forming in a flurry of unsolved murders in London. Patronized by her husband and the police, Susan's insights are given short shrift. She responds to this dismissiveness by calling on her former Bletchley colleagues to solve the crimes.

As the Bletchley Circle collaborates to uncover the murderer of young and vulnerable women, the decipherers' lives are also uncovered. We see that in post war London there is indeed a continuum of violence against women. One of the circle, Lucy, has an incredible eidetic memory. Yet her husband intimidates her to the point of physical abuse. Even Susan, the prime mover of the group, is constricted by her husband's expectations of "proper behavior of a housewife." Rather than see her brilliance, he provides the bushel under which her light shall be hidden. Unable to share with him what she is doing in an effort to stop the murders, she hides her every move. Not the violence of mayhem and murder, no; but snuffing the spirit and life of a soul is an insidious, simmering kind of violence.

The Antidote to Toxic Masculinity

We must recognize that the feminine principle is not the province of women alone. The director of *Osama*, Siddiq

Barmak, is a man of feminine principle. Malala's father, an educator and activist, has always supported his daughter's intelligence and integrity.

As I ponder how patriarchal violence blatantly targets women, I attend a mini-meditation morning with Sharon Salzburg. Almost at the end of her talk, interspersed with meditations, comes the question/comment from a man in the audience who says he is ashamed of what men do to women. His comment was on the heels of the news of the women kept captive in Cleveland for ten years. Prior to the Cleveland story was the reporting of brutal rapes and murders in India. Also in the news was the sexual abuse of women in the military.

Here was a feminine principled man disturbed by the violence men inflict upon women. He would have been appalled at the man enacting the "gossip" at Chadds Ford Days, and if he had overheard the conversation that ensued at the hotdog stand, I believe he would have confronted those men for their unconscionable attitudes.

As deplorable as all these acts of violence to women are, I hope that there is an upwelling of awareness about such violence and that a convergence of consciousness is occurring. The fact that such stories are even talked about in a meditation hall and are addressed by a man indicates, perhaps, that there is an alchemical reaction brewing in the crucible of, not just Western culture, but, dare I say it—"civilization."

HEARTFUL MIND

There is much noise in the world from the right and the left.

Would that we could all take a deep breath and not be led by our limbic systems, that is, our lizard brains. Yes, we sure do need our instinctual brains to get us to remove our hand from a hot stove or to flee a burning building. We don't need it, however, to be the impulsive, reactive leader in conversations with others.

What we do need in dialog is heartful mind. Some may call this mindfulness. But what is mindfulness really, but speaking from the heart connected to our executive functioner, the prefrontal cortex. What if we consider the prefrontal cortex to be the masculine logic and the heartfelt connection to logic to be the feminine feeling function. Yes, this is a simplistic stereotype. However, it might help to understand how we need the balance of the logos and eros, the masculine and feminine in our lives. This is true for both men and women. Everyone needs the balance of the feminine principle and it appears to be what is often so lacking in the cacophony of our culture. Loud times do indeed need the quiet wisdom of the heart of the feminine principle.

The Buddhists say speech needs four elements. One, is what I want to say "true?" Am I speaking my own truth? Two, is it necessary to speak this truth? That is, is this important enough to need to be said? Three, is this the right time to say it? In other words, do I need to take time away from the heat of the moment so the lizard brain isn't the one doing the talking? Four, can what needs to be said, be said with kindness? That means can I say this with compassion without demonizing and objectifying the other person?

There is much noise and shrillness that lacks heartfelt wisdom—there is no heartful mind. We all let our amygdalas get the best of us.

While I write, I sight a great blue heron. I summon my husband to get his camera. The heron lingers close. We stay in stillness with it, even though in the distance jet skiers come with thumping sounds and lots of wake. The heron watches them warily, or am I anthropomorphizing? ... I watch this lake, calm when the heron arrived, churn and splash when a speed boat even a mile away creates a deep wave. I have been swimming here every day, and even when the water is calm, when I hear a power boat in the distance I know the heavy wake will come. It is hard for me to stay centered and keep my breath going.

I need to learn the heavy rhythm of the wave created by these mini-monsters in order to keep my own swim stroke, and breath, even. So it is with the noise of the world, we find our own flow perturbed by the hard wakes created by the loudness and heaviness of mindless reactivity even if it is distant. Perhaps we need to learn how to swim even in such churning waters remembering that the waves eventually subside and that we remain swimming in the flow.

Now, I look up to see two kayakers in the distance. I faintly hear their voices, but there is no boisterous wake.

...

This little book rests on the work of many giant hearts and minds. Certainly there is much that has not been said that needs to be addressed. This last chapter of this book is only the beginning of the journey ahead. Every story I read or hear indicates to me that the tension of the polarities of *status quo* patriarchy and the process to integrate the feminine principle is ongoing.

We courageously face the powers that be. We must remind ourselves not to collapse into the indifference and apathy that allows the patriarchy to continue its violent ways. We must individually and collectively see the interconnection: That violence against women is connected to violence to the Earth is connected to climate change to plutocracy to politics. But it is our collective connection to the feminine principle that can heal the violence. In relationship to one another and to the earth, the wounded feminine shall rise.

Behind the scenes: an Indian woman keeping the hearth fires burning at Saccidananda ashram, Tamil Nadu. May we honor the invisible, anonymous among us who enhance our lives everyday. Indeed, we are interbeings. We are one. *(Photo by the author.)*

AFTERWORD:
MENTORS, MODELS,
AND THE JOURNEY
AHEAD

The greatest challenge of the day is how to bring about a revolution of the heart. A revolution that must start with each one of us. (Dorothy Day)

MENTORS AND MODELS

Recently, Madeleine Albright, former U.S. Secretary of State, spoke at the CIA'a celebration of Women's History Month. Giving career advice to women, she said:

Finally, I have one message that I always insist on sharing with professional women, and that is to look around the room at the faces of your colleagues and remember that there is a special place in Hell reserved for women who refuse to help one another. None of us—none of us get to where we are on our own. And none of us will get to where we want to go unless we move forward together. And if you remember nothing else from what I've said this morning—remember that.

Akin to Albright's comments and closer to home for me is an email I received from Karen Porter, Director of the Chester County (PA) Peace Movement. Allow me to share with you the contents of this email.

The Inquirer recently published a letter I wrote in response to a commentary criticizing Justice Ruth Bader Ginsburg. I received many comments – most complimentary, some very critical, some quite nutty. But this is the best of all – from the Justice herself – to whom one of the readers forwarded my letter:

Dear Karen:
A friend sent me a copy of your Letter to the Editor, published by the Philadelphia Inquirer on March 26. It lifted my spirits. Thanks so much for caring.
R.B.G.

Here's [the] letter:
Editor:
I resent the term "ideologue" as applied to Justice Ruth Bader Ginsburg in the recent commentary in your newspaper ("Accidentally exposing an ideologue," March 20). I met Justice Ginsburg many years before she ascended to the Court, and she was simply the kindest person one could meet. In fact, barely knowing me, she offered to write a recommendation for law school for me (and I took her up on it) out of the kindness of her heart and her concern for women who, at that time, had few rights. She was paving the way for women long before great numbers of women could study law, not only as

a role model, but also as a litigator for our rights. The commentary appeared hostile not only to her work on behalf of women, but to women generally; and I found it totally tone-deaf to women's very real problems – many of which Justice Ginsburg solved. Every woman in this country owes a huge debt to Justice Ginsburg, a fact the commentary callously disregarded. Women matter, and she helped us matter in ways we were denied before her life's work began. She now serves with true ideologues and judicial activists – on the rabid right – and I thank goodness every day she's there speaking for us.

What examples these are of women who are feminine principled mentors and models and supportive of not only women but of both justice and mercy for all.

MENTORS OF MY PAST CARRY ME FORWARD

When I was 15 years old my history and English teacher, Sister David, handed me a book. "Here you might like to read this." she said. It was Dorothy day's memoir, *The Long Loneliness*. This sheltered Catholic schoolgirl was opened to a whole new world of activists and socialist Catholicism that went beyond the blessings, benedictions, incense and Latin litanies that I knew so well. Here was a woman who had a baby out of wedlock, was a journalist and who converted to Catholicism in her adulthood. She found that the Catholic worker movement in the New York City Bowery. What she proselytized and wrote about—social justice for the poor and disenfranchised—she lived. Still too confined as a teen,

I could not imagine myself visiting her in New York. But I did subscribe to her newspaper, the *Catholic Worker*.

It was in reading an article in this publication that I fell in love with my next heroine: Maria Montessori. Here was a woman who in the Victorian era managed to be both a physician and an unwed mother. Where Dorothy Day awakened my sense of social justice, Montessori led me to consider a way of education that was to be a way of peace. Now we see, at least in the US, Montessori schools to be for those who can afford them. But Maria Montessori's first schools were for the disadvantaged children in Italy who were considered mentally challenged. And one of the main tenets of her philosophy was that the collaboration of little children in the school setting could lead to peace in the world.

Teenagers are both self-absorbed and idealistic. I would say that Sister David chose to feed my idealism with her introducing me to Dorothy Day which led me to Maria Montessori.

Somewhere in all this, I also came to love the lithographs of Käthe Kollwitz. Her illustrations of mothers with their children facing death, war and poverty head on touched my heart. No Hallmark moments, these. So too, did Käthe Kollwitz join my women of heart hall of fame.

No venerable Dorothy Day, Sister David, Maria Montessori, or Käthe Kollwitz myself, nevertheless, I hope I still carry in my heart, a place for the idealism they nurtured.

The Journey Ahead and Questions to Ponder

- Who are your mentors? Who are your models of the feminine principle?
- Where do you notice the feminine principle rising?
- Where do you notice the feminine principle's burial, and the pushback from the patriarchal powers that be?
- What ways can you observe the culture, the media, world events, and consider where are the men and women of heart who in their actions reflect the feminine principle?
- Where has the feminine principle been wounded in you?
- Where is the feminine principle rising in you?
- How might you carry forward into the world a way in which the feminine principle can be nurtured? Is it through environmental action? Political action? Personal change?

The more awareness we have of ourselves, the more an awakening consciousness we have about the rise of the wounded feminine in the midst of a world of domination and violence, the more the feminine principle can be acknowledged as the sustainer of life on earth. What if we thought of the feminine principle as the womb of the world—life-giving nurturer and protector of new creation?

A LITANY OF HEART

From the Invocation to Kali (my Pele) by May Sarton:

Help us to be the always hopeful
Gardeners of the spirit
Who know that without darkness
Nothing comes to birth
As without light
Nothing flowers.
   Bear the roots in mind,
You, the dark one, Kali,
Awesome power.

Heart of Dorothy Day, help us to be unconventional in our seeking beauty.

Heart of Amy Goodman, help us to speak truth to power.

Heart of Käthe Kollwitz, help us to transform our grief and pain into creative new life.

Heart of Marian Anderson, help us to sing the story of our hearts.

Heart of Abigail Adams, helps us to send letters of love (as you did to John Adams) that help transform the ways of the world.

241

Heart of Shirley Chisholm, help us to stand up to men of power, even our enemies, with a compassionate heart, as you did with George Wallace.

Heart of Virginia Satir, help us to be strong and unique in our individuality guiding our families to open and honest communication.

Hearts of Maria Montessori and Mr. Rogers, help us to know how to honor our children by being with them right where they are.

Heart of Miriam Greenspan, help us to heal our dark emotions, not by running away from them, but by honest and gentle encounter with them.

Heart of Marian Woodman, help us to honor and cherish our bodies in all our outward shapes and forms.

Heart of Helen Luke, help us to "lick the sores" and to face the world with courage.

Heart of Clarissa Pinkola Estés, help us to honor the wolf energy within.

Hearts of writers, such as Maxine Hong Kingston, Alice Walker, Stieg Larsson, Riane Eisler, Bill Moyers, Chris Hedges, Dave Zirin, help us to come to awareness through your words.

Heart of Frederick Douglas, help us to find the courage to move from awareness to right action.

Hearts of brave young women, such as Malala, help us not to be silenced even in our woundedness.

Heart of Martin Luther King, help us to see beyond our prejudices how we are interconnected.

Heart of Thich Nhat Hanh, help us to live in "interbeing" in the world.

Hearts of Joanna Macy, Rachel Carson, Wangari Maathai, help us to care for our mother, Earth.

Hearts of Richard Rohr, David Richo, Donald Kalsched, James Hollis, Robert Johnson, help us be seekers of psychospiritual wisdom.

Hearts of physicians, such as Paul Farmer and Michael Phillips, help us care for the medical needs of the anonymous and forgotten.

Hearts of Russill Paul, and Bede Griffiths before him, help us to integrate the spirituality of East and West, female and male.

Hearts of poets, such as Naomi Shihab Nye, Mary Oliver, Wendell Berry, David Whyte, help us know the transcendent in the immanent.

Hearts of our grandmothers, mothers, teachers, help us to find our own wisdom and our own way to transform the world.

Hearts of all our ancestors lead us to peace and light.

There are many men and women, of course, not mentioned here, who are our mentors and guides also. This could be an infinite prayer! Reflect now on those you would add to your litany of heart.

BIBLIOGRAPHY

A Dangerous Method. Dir. David Cronenberg. Sony Pictures Classics, 2011, Film.

Abuelaish, Izzeldin. *I Shall Not Hate.* New York: Walker & Company, 2010.

Albright, Madeleine. Excerpts of Remarks Delivered at the CIA Women's History Month Celebration. *Central Intelligence Agency.* <http://www.foia.cia.gov/sites/default/files/document_conversions/1820853/2013-03-22.pdf>. 19 March 2013.

Arsenault, Raymond. *The Sound of Freedom.* New York: Bloomsbury Press, 2009.

Ayres, Ed. "The Banality of Evil." *World Watch* Jan-Feb 1998, p. 3.

Barlett, Donald L. and James B. Steele. *The Betrayal of the American Dream.* New York: Public Affairs, 2012.

Berry, Thomas. *The Dream of the Earth,* Sierra Club Books, 2nd ed., 2006.

Bolen, Jean Shinoda. *Goddesses in Every Woman.* New York: Harper & Row, 1985;

Gods in Every Man. New York: Harper & Row, 1989.

Burns, Jennifer, *Goddess of the Market: Ayn Rand and the*

American Right. New York: Oxford University Press, 2009.

Chalquist, Craig. "Archetype." *A Glossary of Jungian Terms*, <http://terrapsych.com/jungdefs.html>. Accessed 16 February 2014.

Chittister, Joan. "Tainted by 'radical feminism'? More like 'living the Gospel.'" *National Catholic Reporter*, May 10-23, 2013, p. 30.

Claremont de Castillejo, Irene. *Knowing Woman*. New York: Harper & Row, 1973.

Clifton, Lucille, Kevin Young, *et al*, eds. *The Collected Poems of Lucille Clifton 1965-2010*. Rochester, NY: Boa Editions, Ltd, 2012.

Coffey, Kathy. *Women of Mercy*. New York: Orbis, 2005.

Cole, Susan, Ronan, Marian and Taussig, Hal. *Wisdom's Feast: Sophia in Study and Celebration*. New York: Harper & Row, 1986.

Dinnerstein, Dorothy. *The Mermaid and the Minotaur: Sexual Arrangements and Human Malaise*. New York: Harper & Row, 1976.

Douglas, Susan (with Sady Doyle). "Feminism...What's Next?" *In These Times*, August, 2012.

Ecenbarger, William. *Kids for Cash: Two Judges, Thousands of Children, and a $2.6 Million Kickback Scheme*. New York: The New Press, 2012.

Edinger, Edward. *Anatomy of the Psyche*. Chicago: Open Court, 1994.

Eisler, Riane. *The Chalice and the Blade: Our History, Our Future*. New York: HarperOne, 1988;

The Power of Partnership: Seven Relationships that Will Change Your Life. Novato, CA: New World Library, 2003; *The Real Wealth of Nations: Creating a Caring Economics.* San Francisco: Berrett-Koehler Publishers, 2008; *Sacred Pleasure: Sex, Myth, and the Politics of the Body—New Paths to Power and Love.* HarperOne, 1996; *Women, Men, and the Global Quality of Life.* Center for Partnership Studies,1995

Estés, Clarissa Pinkola. *Untie the Strong Woman: Blessed Mother's Immaculate Love for the Wild Soul.* Boulder, CO: Sounds True, Inc, 2011; *Women Who Run With the Wolves.* New York: Ballantine, 1992.

Fey, Tina. *Bossypants.* Back Bay Books, 2012.

Gabrielson, Eva. *"There Are Things I Want You to Know" About Stieg Larsson and Me,* New York: Seven Stories Press, 2011.

Gajdos, Kathleen. "Everyday Compassion: Mr. Rogers and Kathe Kollwitz." *Illness, Crisis, and Loss,* 12:3 (2004): 223-230; "The Intergenerational Effects of Grief and Trauma." *Illness, Crisis, and Loss,* 10:4 (2002): 304-317.

Gilligan, Carol. *In a Different Voice: Psychological Theory and Women's Development.* Cambridge, MA: Harvard University Press, 1982.

Gimbutas, Marija. *The Language of the Goddess.* New York: Harper San Francisco. 1989.

Glass, Ira. *This American Life,* Show 459, March 2, 2012.

Greenspan, Miriam. *Healing Through the Dark Emotions.* Boston: Shambhala, 2003.

Griffin, Susan. *Woman and Nature: The Roaring Inside Her.* Sierra Club Books, Reissue Ed., 2000.

Harris, Maria. *Dance of the Spirit: The Seven Stages of Women's Spirituality.* New York: Bantam Books, 1989; *Jubilee Time.* New York: Bantam Books, 1996.

Harris, Maxine. *Sisters of the Shadow.* Oklahoma: University of Oklahoma Press, 1991.

Hanh, Thich Nhat. *Interbeing: Fourteen Guidelines for Engaged Buddhism.* Parallelax Press, 1987.

Herman, Judith. *Trauma and Recovery: The Aftermath of Violence–from Domestic Abuse to Political Terror.* Basic Books, 1997.

Hollis, James. *Hauntings: Dispelling the Ghosts Who Run Our Lives.* Chiron Pubs, 2013; *On This Journey We Call Our Life: Living the Questions.* Toronto: Inner City Books, 2003; *Under Saturn's Shadow: The Wounding and Healing of Men.* Toronto: Inner City Books, 1994; *What Matters Most: Living a More Considered Life.* Gotham, 2008.

Hvistendahl, Mara. *Unnatural Selection: Choosing Boys Over Girls, and the Consequences of a World Full of Men.* New York: BBS, Public Affairs, 2011.

Jacobi, Jolande. *Psychological Reflections: An Anthology of the Writings of C. G. Jung.* New York: Harper & Row, 1953.

Johnson, Robert. *Femininity Lost and Regained.* New York: Harper & Row, 1990;

He: Understanding Masculine Psychology. New York: Harper & Row, 1977;

Inner Gold. Kihei, HI: Koa Books (2008);

She: Understanding Feminine Psychology. Berkeley: Mills House, 1989;

We: Understanding the Psychology of Romantic Love. New York: Harper Collins, 1983.

Jung, C. G. *The Collected Works of C. G. Jung.* Edited by Sir Herbert Read, Michael Fordham, Gerhard Adler and William McGuire. Translated by R. F. C. Hull (except for Vol. 2) New York/Princeton (Bollingen Series XX) and London, 1953-76;

Vol. 5. *Symbols of Transformation.* 1967;

Vol. 6. *Psychological Types.* 1971;

Vol. 9, Part 1. *The Archetypes and the Collective Unconscious.* 1968;

Vol. 9, Part 2. *Aion: Researches into the Phenomenology of the Self.* 1968;

Vol. 10. *Civilization in Transition.* 1970;

Vol.18. *The Symbolic Life: Miscellaneous Writings.* 1975;

Jung, Emma. *Animus and Anima.* Woodstock, Connecticut: Spring Publications, 1985.

Kalsched, Donald. *Trauma and the Soul: A psycho-spiritual approach to human development and its interruption.* Taylor & Francis, 2013.

Khamisa, Azim N. *Azim's Bardo – From Murder to Forgiveness – A Father's Journey.* Bloomington, IN: Balboa Press, 2012.

Kingston, Maxine Hong. *The Woman Warrior: Memoirs of a Girlhood Among Ghosts.* New York: Random House, 1976.

Kingston, Maxine Hong (ed). *Veterans of War, Veterans of Peace*. Kihei, HI: Koa Books, 2006.

Kristof, Nicholas D. & WuDunn, Sheryl. *Half the Sky: Turning Oppression into Opportunity for Women Worldwide*. New York: Knopf, 2009.

Larsson, Stieg. *The Girl with the Dragon Tattoo*. New York: Vintage, 2009;
The Girl Who Played With Fire. New York: Vintage, 2010;
The Girl Who Kicked the Hornet's Nest. New York: Knopf, 2010.

Levine, Peter. *Healing Trauma: A Pioneering Program for Restoring the Wisdom of Your Body*. Sounds True, Inc., 2008.

Levine, Stephen. *A Gradual Awakening*. Anchor, 1989;
Healing into Life and Death. Anchor, 1989.

de Llosa, Patty, *Taming Your Inner Tyrant*. Holmdell, NJ: A Spiritual Evolution Press, 2011.

Lopez-Corvo, Rafael E. *God Is a Woman*. Northvale, NJ: Jason Aronson, 1997.

Luke, Helen. *The Way of Woman*. New York: Doubleday, 1995.

Macy, Joanna. *World as Lover, World as Self: Courage for Global Justice and Ecological Renewal*. Berkeley, CA: Parallax Press, 2007.

Marlan, Stanton. *The Black Sun: The Alchemy and Art of Darkness*. Texas: Texas A&M University Press, 2005.

Mazur, Allan, and Joel Michalek. "Marriage, Divorce, And Male Testosterone." *Social Forces* 77.1 (1998): 315-330.

Miller, Jean Baker. *Toward a New Psychology of Women*. Boston: Beacon Press, 1986.

Moore, Thomas. *Care of the Soul: A Guide for Cultivating Depth and Sacredness in Everyday Life.* New York: Harper Collins, 1992.

Naidoo, Kumi. Interviewed by Amy Goodman, *DemocracyNow.org*, December 10, 2012.

Neumann, Erich. *Depth Psychology and a New Ethic.* Boston: Shambhala, 1990.

Oliver, Mary, *A Thousand Mornings.* New York: The Penguin Press, 2012.

Paul, Russill. *Yoga of Sound.* Novato, CA: New World Library, 2004.

Perera, Sylvia. *Descent to the Goddess.* Toronto: Inner City Books, 1981.

Pollitt, Katha. Interviewed by Sady Doyle and Susan J. Douglas. *In These Times*, August, 2012.

Pozner, Jennifer L. *Reality Bites Back: The Troubling Truth About Guilty Pleasure TV.* Berkeley: Seal Press, 2010.

Rich, Adrienne. *Of Woman Born.* New York: W.W. Norton & Co., 1976.

Richo, David. *Mary Within Us: A Jungian Contemplation of Her Titles and Powers.* New York: Crossroad, 2001; *Shadow Dance: Liberating the Power & Creativity of Your Dark Side.* Boston: Shambhala Publications, 1999.

Rieder, Jonathan. *Gospel of Freedom.* New York: Bloomsbury Press, 2013.

Robinson, Sara, www.alternet.org, "Why Patriarchal Men are Utterly Petrified of Birth Control—And Why We'll Still Be Fighting About it 100 Years From Now," February 15, 2012.

Rohr, Richard. *Following Upward*. San Francisco: Jossey-Bass, 2011.

(and Joseph Martos) *From Wild Man to Wise Man: Reflections on Male Spirituality*. Cincinnati, OH: St Anthony Messenger Press, 2005;

Immortal Diamond: The Search for Our True Self. San Francisco: Jossey-Bass, 2013;

The Naked Now: Learning to See as the Mystics See. The Crossroad Publishing Company, 2006;

On the Threshold of Transformation: Daily Meditations for Men. Loyola Press, 2010.

Ruddick, Sara. *Maternal Thinking: Toward a Politics of Peace*. Boston: Beacon Press, 1995.

Sardello, Robert. *Love and the Soul: Creating a Future for Earth*. New York: Harper Perennial, 1996.

Schireson, Grace. *Zen Women: Beyond Tea Ladies, Iron Maidens, and Macho Masters*. Boston: Wisdom Publications, 2009.

Sharp, Daryl. *Jung Lexicon: A Primer of Terms and Concepts*. Toronto: Inner City Books, 1990.

Smith, Samantha. Interviewed by Amy Goodman. *DemocracyNow.org*, December 10, 2012.

Starhawk. *Dreaming the Dark*. Boston: Beacon Press, 1982.

Steingraber, Sandra. *Living Downstream: An Ecologist's Personal Investigation of Cancer and the Environment*. London: Virago Press, 1997.

Tannen, Deborah. *You Just Don't Understand: Women and Men in Conversation*. William Morrow Paperbacks, 2007.

Verghese, Abraham. *Cutting for Stone*. New York: Random House, 2009.

von Franz, Marie Louise. *C. G. Jung: His Myth in Our Time*. New York: G. P. Putnam's Sons, 1975; *Psyche and Matter*. Boston: Shambhala Publications, 1992.

Walker, Alice. *The Color Purple*. New York: Washington Square, 1983; *The World Will Follow Joy*. New York: The New Press, 2013.

Walker, Barbara G. *The Crone: Woman of Age, Wisdom and Power*. New York: Harper & Row, 1985.

Wellstone, Paul, *The Conscience of a Liberal: Reclaiming the Agenda*. Minneapolis: University of Minnesota Press, 2002.

Whitmont, Edward C. *Return of the Goddess*. New York: The Crossroad Publishing Co, 1982.

Wink, Walter. *The Powers That Be: Theology for a New Millennium*. New York: Galilee Doubleday, 1998.

Wise, Tim. *Speaking Treason Fluently: Anti-Racist Reflections From an Angry White Male*. Berkeley, CA: Soft Skull Press, 2008.

Woodman, Marion & Dickson, Elinor. *Dancing in the Flames: The Dark Goddess in the Transformation of Consciousness*. Boston: Shambhala Publications, 1996.

Worthington, Everett L. *Forgiving and Reconciling: Bridges to Wholeness and Hope*. Downers Grove, IL: Intervarsity Press, 2003.

Young-Bruehl, Elisabeth. *Hannah Arendt: For Love of the World*. New Haven: Yale University Press, 2nd edition, 2004.

Young-Bruehl, Elisabeth, and Faith Bethelard. Cherishment: *A Psychology of the Heart*. New York: The Free Press, 2000.

Young-Eisendrath, Polly & Dawson, Terence. *The Cambridge Companion to Jung*. Cambridge, UK: Cambridge University Press, 1997.

Zirin, Dave. *Game Over: How Politics Has Turned the Sports World Upside Down*. New York: The New Press, 2013.

ACKNOWLEDGEMENTS

There is no way I can ever list all the people for whom I am heartfully grateful. So many anonymous people have touched my life. Their kindness has been part of my journey.

For example, I remember the policewoman who, with her male partner, escorted us to the hospital ER after they stopped us for "speeding." Cautioning me not to get out of the car, she gave me hope with her words: "Let me get the wheelchair, you don't know that this is a miscarriage." Her kindness buoyed me through the night, and I never forgot her. Indeed, the pregnancy was tenuous and at risk for months, but my son did make it through.

Such stories of kindness from strangers could fill another book.

I need also to acknowledge my family of origin: my mother for her endurance and grace; my father for his gentleness and love of words and grammar; my brother, Bill, for his care for the environment; Uncle Frank and Aunt Mary for being non-judgmental quiet presences; Father Edmund for his protection and beneficence; Aunt Helen for her intelligence; my straight-backed grandmother for her stolidness and warmth.

I am grateful for the teachers of my past: Sr. Julienne, Sr. Benedicta, Sr. David, Peter Frank. Dear friends, such as Evasio de Marcellis and John Opalek, for their kindness.

I heartily thank Barry Panter for providing the opportunity at *Creativity and Madness* seminars to present my work on the Stieg Larsson trilogy as well as on the Rise of the Wounded Feminine in the Media. Those experiences were crucial to the writing of this book.

I thank Debbie Cirilli for her patience and administrative skills; Kyle Lanier for keeping me moving; Mariah Martin, Chris Eckery and Marlene Smith for their intuitive midwifery; Bruce Cryer for his early support of my writing endeavor; Marion Sandmaier for her encouragement and initial editing guidance; Henry S.T. for keeping me rooted through the process; friends Perry and Dirk for giving me an opportunity to write at the lake; research librarians Heidi, Bill, and Catherine at St. Joseph's University; Dick Swaine and his staff at West Chester University library; Talula's Table and staff for being just the "write" café; Martha Turner and Cliff Smith for their encouragement.

And, of course, I thank my daughter, Zofia, for her help, especially with the Larsson trilogy, and for embodying wonder woman herself; son-in-law Matt Meuse and best friend "brother" Victor Lum for allowing me to tag along to Acadia National Park where I wrote and they camped. I thank my husband Larry for his abiding love and support and his indispensable computer and word processing savvy. I have infinite gratitude for my son, Johnathan, who embodies the feminine principle in remarkable ways and whose publishing expertise was essential in bringing this book to fruition.

And, to all the friends and family not mentioned here, a deep bow to everyone.

ABOUT THE AUTHOR

Dr. Kayta (Kathleen) Curzie Gajdos is a psychologist who works with individuals, couples, and families. She has experience and training in the fields of alcohol and drug addictions, hypnosis, family therapy, Jungian theory, meditation and mindfulness, grief and trauma, EMDR, ETT, sandplay therapy, and dreamwork. Dr. Gajdos developed a practice in the Pittsburgh area, where she also wrote for the Western Psychiatric Institute and Clinic's *Family Therapy Newsletter*.

Dr. Gajdos has published in the American Psychological Association *Bulletin*, *The Family Psychologist*, and in the Swedenborgian publications, *Chrysalis* and *The Messenger*. *Illness, Crisis and Loss* has published her articles on intergenerational grief as well as on the compassion of Käthe Kollwitz and Mr. Rogers. She has taught at the graduate level at West Chester University and Wilmington University, and has supervised psychologists in training. Having served as field faculty for Vermont College of Norwich University and the Union Institute's Center for Distance Learning, she most recently served as external faculty for Pacifica Graduate Institute.

Living in Chadds Ford, Pennsylvania, Dr. Gajdos has been a columnist for the Chadds Ford Post and the Kennett

Paper. Now, her *Mind Matters* column appears online in *Chadds Ford Live*. In addition to her private practice, Dr. Gajdos facilitates a grief support group, SAM (Survivors of Accident and Murder) for the Mental Health Association in Delaware. Active in disaster relief with the Red Cross and Medical Reserve Corps, she is the Disaster Resource Network coordinator for the Delaware Psychological Association. She participated in Hurricane Katrina relief efforts as a member of teams from the Department of Health and Human Services' Substance Abuse and Mental Health Services Administration (SAMHSA).

In the past, she has led workshops at Temenos Retreat Center on themes such as inter-generational grief, meditation, the shadow, and shame. She also facilitated numerous times a "Griefs of Birthing" ritual for those who suffered losses of procreation (abortions, miscarriages, infertility, etc.). Most recently, Dr. Gajdos has been a presenter at several *Creativity and Madness* Conferences, as well as the Won Institute and the Community for Integrative Learning (in Wilmington, Delaware).

She is a member of the American Family Therapy Academy, the American Psychological Association, the Delaware Psychological Association, the Pennsylvania Psychological Association, the Association for Death Education and Counseling, International Society of Traumatic Stress Studies, Emotional Transformation Therapy International Association, and the EMDR International Association.

She serves on the Delaware County Mental Health and Intellectual Disabilities Advisory Board, and on the Board of Governors of the Greater Philadelphia Society of Clinical Hypnosis, as well. Woven into her professional career, she is active in walking, swimming, dancing, and writing.

CPSIA information can be obtained at www.ICGtesting.com
Printed in the USA
BVOW03s1737250414

351479BV00002B/27/P